NEW ESSAYS ON THE SCARLET LETTER

★ The American Novel ★

GENERAL EDITOR

Emory Elliott, *Princeton University*

Other books in the series:
New Essays on The Great Gatsby
New Essays on Adventures of Huckleberry Finn

Forthcoming:
New Essays on Chopin's The Awakening (ed. Wendy Martin)
New Essays on The Red Badge of Courage (ed. Lee Mitchell)
New Essays on Ellison's Invisible Man (ed. Robert O'Meally)
New Essays on Light in August (ed. Michael Millgate)
New Essays on The Sun Also Rises (ed. Linda Wagner)
New Essays on James's The American (ed. Martha Banta)
New Essays on Moby-Dick (ed. Richard Brodhead)
New Essays on Uncle Tom's Cabin (ed. Eric Sundquist)

New Essays on
The Scarlet Letter

Edited by
Michael J. Colacurcio

The right of the
University of Cambridge
to print and sell
all manner of books
was granted by
Henry VIII in 1534.
The University has printed
and published continuously
since 1584.

CAMBRIDGE UNIVERSITY PRESS

Cambridge

New York   New Rochelle

Melbourne   Sydney

Published by the Press Syndicate of the University of Cambridge
The Pitt Building, Trumpington Street, Cambridge CB2 1RP
32 East 57th Street, New York, NY 10022, USA
10 Stamford Road, Oakleigh, Melbourne 3166, Australia

First published 1985
Reprinted 1986, 1988

Printed in the United States of America

Library of Congress Cataloging in Publication Data
Main entry under title:
New essays on The scarlet letter.
(The American novel)
Bibliography: p.
1. Hawthorne, Nathaniel, 1804–1864. Scarlet letter
–Addresses, essays, lectures.   1. Colacurcio, Michael.
II. Series.
PS1868.N48   1985   813'.3   85–7810
ISBN 0 521 26676 9 hard covers
ISBN 0 521 31998 6 paperback

(M)

Contents

v

Contents

Series Editor's Preface

IN literary criticism the last twenty-five years have been particularly fruitful. Since the rise of the New Criticism in the 1950s, which focused attention of critics and readers upon the text itself–apart from history, biography, and society–there has emerged a wide variety of critical methods which have brought to literary works a rich diversity of perspectives: social, historical, political, psychological, economic, ideological, and philosophical. While attention to the text itself, as taught by the New Critics, remains at the core of contemporary interpretation, the widely shared assumption that works of art generate many different kinds of interpretation has opened up possibilities for new readings and new meanings.

Before this critical revolution, many American novels had come to be taken for granted by earlier generations of readers as having an established set of recognized interpretations. There was a sense among many students that the canon was established and that the larger thematic and interpretative issues had been decided. The task of the new reader was to examine the ways in which elements such as structure, style, and imagery contributed to each novel's acknowledged purpose. But recent criticism has brought these old assumptions into question and has thereby generated a wide variety of original, and often quite surprising, interpretations of the classics, as well as of rediscovered novels such as Kate Chopin's *The Awakening,* which has only recently entered the canon of works that scholars and critics study and that teachers assign their students.

The aim of The American Novel Series is to provide students of American literature and culture with introductory critical guides to

American novels now widely read and studied. Each volume is devoted to a single novel and begins with an introduction by the volume editor, a distinguished authority on the text. The introduction presents details of the novel's composition, publication history, and contemporary reception, as well as a survey of the major critical trends and readings from first publication to the present. This overview is followed by four or five original essays, specifically commissioned from senior scholars of established reputation and from outstanding younger critics. Each essay presents a distinct point of view, and together they constitute a forum of interpretative methods and of the best contemporary ideas on each text.

It is our hope that these volumes will convey the vitality of current critical work in American literature, generate new insights and excitement for students of the American novel, and inspire new respect for and new perspectives upon these major literary texts.

Emory Elliott
Princeton University

1

Introduction:
The Spirit and the Sign

MICHAEL J. COLACURCIO

1

UNLESS one insists on counting *Fanshawe* (1828), which the author never would entirely own, *The Scarlet Letter* (1850) is Hawthorne's first "extended" fiction. Whether one names it "novel" or "romance" – and however one decides the vexed question of its true relation to its "Custom-House" introduction – the fact remains that it represents a significant new departure in a well-established literary career. Not thematically, of course, since its interest in the inner life and symbols of the American Puritans is well forecast by some of Hawthorne's earliest and most powerful writings; apparently that matter lay always within reach. But generically, *The Scarlet Letter* is a first indeed: Somehow an accomplished master of the highly compressed "tale" and the barely elaborated "sketch" was able to make a single story fill up a whole book. And somehow, even more surprisingly, that book turned out to be his one undisputed masterpiece of world literature. Perhaps we should review the conditions surrounding his not quite predictable innovation and triumph.[1]

About a number of these conditions, "The Custom-House" exists to provide the definitive statement. The life Hawthorne had lived at Concord's famous Old Manse (from 1842 to 1845), and the tales he gathered together as its literary memorial, were now far enough behind him to seem a little unreal. The man who had known the perfect Platonism of Bronson Alcott (and who had struggled to express both the spiritual urgency and the psychic peril of a variety of contemporary transcendentalisms) was now quite firmly established in the world of indubitable facts. The faithful devotee of (American) literary art had been judged the worthy recipient, yet found himself to be as well the victim, of political patronage. And the seeker of spiritual laws had become an inspector of commercial goods.

The identity was puzzling, but the life seemed secure. More secure than it actually was, of course, as the election of 1848 proved that *nobody* was above party politics. Yet the political issue was scarcely the worst of the human case. For the very security – or was it merely the routine? – of the worldly situation seemed inimical to the artistic faculty. Perhaps the "wizard hand" was losing its magic touch.

In the years following his appointment, in April 1846, as Surveyor of the Revenue in the Salem Custom-House, Hawthorne had written, by his own standards at least, very little indeed: a handful of literary reviews (for a *Whig* paper, as it painfully came to appear), a tale of the "unpardonable sin" called "Ethan Brand" (itself quite possibly but a fragment of some "abortive romance"), and perhaps the beginnings of an historical sketch called "Main Street" (full of weighty themes but noticeably lacking in dramatic intensity). By contrast, the Concord phase had yielded up nearly two dozen tales and sketches, so that the original edition of *Mosses from an Old Manse* (1846) needed to contain little else. And back at the origins, of course, the Salem years had produced a bibliography of some seventy-five items – more than enough to fill three crescive editions of *Twice-told Tales* (1837, 1842, 1851). To be sure, the present literary lapse was not altogether unprecedented. In the years between Salem and Concord (1839–41), when Hawthorne held his first Custom-House position (in Boston), and during his ill-starred experiment at Brook Farm, his literary output also slowed. Yet this precedent was scarcely encouraging. It might require a final experiment (the service as Consul to Liverpool, 1853–7) to convince literary historians that episodes of politics inevitably divide Hawthorne's career into its several neat phases; but already it fairly appeared that Hawthorne could not write imaginative literature and do worldly work at the same time.

Thus it is impossible, finally, to be *too* sorry about Hawthorne's political ouster, however bitter the satire of "The Custom-House" sometimes becomes. Nor should we worry too much about the sour-grapes inconsistency by which he tries to persuade himself and us that unemployment was what he really wanted. Clearly, Hawthorne wanted both worldly security and imaginative challenge. When the world (once again) denied him the one, there was no choice except to face (once again) the other.

And so, sometime in the second half of 1849 (he was notified of his removal on July 8), Hawthorne went back to living by his pen alone. By September he was writing so "immensely" that his wife was almost frightened. "The Great Stone Face" was ready for the January 1850 number of the *National Era*; "The Custom-House" and all but the last three chapters of what came to be called *The Scarlet Letter* were in the hands of a publisher by January 15, 1850; and "The Snow-Image," although it did not appear until October 1850, was also written (or completed) at about this same time. Evidently Hawthorne *could* still write, when he had to.

Yet the thematic variety and artistic variance of these works indicate just how uninevitable *The Scarlet Letter* really was. Whatever autobiographical experience may be encoded in the famous fiction of finding, in the upper room of the Custom-House, the faded letter, and also a manuscript version of the life and not-quite-Christian conversation of Hester Prynne, and of accepting, from the ghost of Mr. Surveyor Pue, the spiritual duty of writing up the affair in his own chosen mode, the thing clearly did not write itself. The legend that Mrs. Hawthorne greeted the news of her husband's dismissal with the reassurance that now he could write "his book" creates entirely the wrong impression. For what Hawthorne clearly had in mind during the last months of 1849 was not a single fiction that might stand defiantly alone, but rather a collection of the various works he had managed recently to produce, supplemented perhaps by some older materials, and introduced (in the manner of the *Mosses*) by yet another chapter of his own quite local though highly fictionalized autobiography. And this in spite of the fact that "The Old Manse" had solemnly announced itself as "the last collection of this kind which it is my purpose ever to put forth." But since the romance "Ethan Brand" had indeed proved abortive, there appeared to be no alternative to a volume entitled "Old-Time Legends; Together with Sketches, Experimental and Ideal."

Apparently it was Hawthorne's publisher, James T. Fields, whose sensibility determined that the elongated "tale" of Hester Prynne, along with the account of its teller's own recent vicissitudes, might constitute a volume by themselves; that the reading public would consider that combined performance lengthy enough to justify its purchase; and that satire and the humor of the introduction would sufficiently relieve the uniform somberness of Hawthorne's latest retreat into the matter of the Puritans. We cannot be certain if the planned collection ever had a firm table of contents, although "Ethan Brand," "The Great Stone Face," and "The Snow-Image" immediately suggest themselves. And the reader will surely notice that the reference to an "article entitled 'Main Street,' included in the present volume" was never edited out of the final text of "The Custom-House." Perhaps the literary history of certain organic unities remains to be written.

But the point is not to undo any or all theories of the larger literary function of Hawthorne's introductory sketch. Such things work if they work, whether they appeared inevitable beforehand or not. It is merely to stress the openness of Hawthorne's literary situation in 1849 and to indicate that "The Custom-House" may not tell us *all* we need to know about how to approach the single and original work Hawthorne published, on March 16, 1850, as *The Scarlet Letter*. Its famous (and highly stylized) language of moonlight, romance, ghosts, and "neutral territory" may not inevitably limit the terms we choose in discussing its literary epistemology. And even its central fiction of an authorial discovery of "the capital letter A" may provide only elementary instruction in how to read the various "signs" – of sin and of life – in the tangled career of Hester Prynne, her scientific husband, and her puritanic lover. It may not even tell us all we need to know about how to identify the voice that tells their tale.

"The Custom-House" tells us that an author anxious about his art is thrown back on his own resources. Formally, of course, these resources are indicated to be the powers of imagination. And materially – as the unexcised reference to "Main Street" also plainly suggests – they are the terms of moral experience in the once intense but now faded world of American Puritanism, even as they were failing to bear the scrutiny of their own users. But what the most crucial of these terms were, exactly, Hawthorne's famous "preface" does not pretend to declare. Unless the manuscript of Mr. Surveyor Pue provides the key to some allegory as yet altogether undeciphered, it leaves the discovery of these to its own more dramatic sequel. And although it suggests that we must make our own translation of them, just as our modern author has translated the terms of Pue's original translation, it does not at all tell us how to do this. Or even if we can expect to be any more than approximately successful: love always burns, no doubt; but letters all fade, and signs may well outlive the thing they signified.

In the end, "The Custom-House" does not even tell us how much of the hidden life of the recently released writer it may be appropriate to look for – resisting intimacy even as it invites a certain sympathetic familiarity. Does his own bitter political experience matter, to the historical plot or the contemporary point of view? Has the career of his own troubled imagination (fascinated, apparently, by the complex topic of private sin and public shame) sought its correlative in the fictional objects of his passionate concern? Will any other equally veiled realities find their silent expression in a tale made up from some hints of history? His marriage, for example? His view of the "woman question"? Or the recent, painful, and faith-tempting death (on July 30, 1849) of his mother? Certain styles of criticism may attempt to invalidate these sorts of questions, of course; but since they do occur, from time to time, to basically earnest and fair-minded readers, it may be a mistake to read them out of court entirely. They are there if they are there, whatever bias "The Custom-House" manages to create. And "criticism" might be defined as the task of trying to answer, however it can, whatever questions will occur to readers.

2

The earliest criticism of *The Scarlet Letter* is likely to strike the eager modern student of literature as somewhat elementary. Mrs. Hawthorne registered her response to her husband's private reading by going "to bed with a grievous headache." And although Hawthorne himself might regard this, half-humorously, as a "triumphant success," he nevertheless worried that the book was indeed "too sombre," its dark shadows entirely unrelieved by any redemptive light beyond. Scrupling that his readers might conceive too gloomy an image of the author himself, he would deliberately set out to make his next long fiction – *The House of the Seven Gables* (1851) – a fairer mixture of guilt and hope. He even expressed a preference for that work (specifically identified as a "romance") on the ground that its moral (and perhaps generic) balance was "more characteristic" of his mind, "more proper and natural" for a man like him to write. Evidently he felt that "The Custom-House" had not entirely done its office.

Striving to lighten up the whole affair, its author had boldly protested (without entire candor, perhaps) that "a better book than I shall ever write" was always suggesting itself in the daily round of Custom-House activity. Yet he wrote what he wrote; and a story that had begun with the hope that "some sweet moral blossom" might be found along the way, "to relieve the darkening close of a tale of human frailty and sorrow," had ended by discovering only "one ever-glowing point of light gloomier than the sorrow." Herman Melville might have helped the author on this point, since his (August 1850) review of "Hawthorne and His Mosses" addresses precisely this primitive question of light and shadow. But its entire critical attention is devoted to the stories included in the *Mosses;* nor do any of Melville's letters, which famously follow up this first personal and literary advance, ever address the question of *The Scarlet Letter* directly. Possibly the two men would go on to discuss the point in the night-time conversations that appear to epitomize their brief but intense period of near neighborhood; but all that Melville can tell the less privileged student of Hawthorne is that there may be deep reasons – theological as well as psychic – why it was not entirely "proper" for Hawthorne to "give us a ray of light for every shade of . . . dark."[2]

Yet if Melville's address to Hawthorne was indeed privileged, his terms of analysis were not precisely prescient. For the original reviews of *The Scarlet Letter* had already raised Hawthorne's own proleptic objection. Not as a damning fault, to be sure, for the critical response to his first long fiction was predominantly favorable.[3] Hawthorne would complain, in his preface to the *Twice-told Tales* of 1851, that he had once been, and for quite a while remained, "the obscurest man of letters in America"; but that era had lapsed long since, and most of the age's leading critics were eager to proclaim that a great writer had surpassed even himself. Still, a prominent British reviewer wondered whether fiction needed to dwell so much on "passions and tragedies." And America's own E. P. Whipple – who may indeed have been prescient, and whose views subsequently influenced Hawthorne's very noticeably – tempered his great enthusiasm with a complaint about a certain "morbid intensity" in the realization of character; and he concluded his review by hoping that Hawthorne's *next* romance would indeed be relieved by more of Hawthorne's "beautiful and peculiar humor."

Most of Hawthorne's reviewers mentioned "The Custom-House," and most were impressed with its satiric sketches, even as these continued to keep the case of the Decapitated Surveyor alive and nasty in the political press, especially in the author's native Salem. Hawthorne's one-time Brook Farm associate, George Ripley, who surely had had personal experience with Hawthorne's capacity for taking care of himself, complained of the book's excessively sharp "touches of the caustic acid, of which the gentle author keeps some phials on his shelf for convenience and use." But most observers thought the local politicos got no more than they deserved. Reviewers tended to see the two "parts" of Hawthorne's latest literary offering as complementary, in setting and in moral tone, but none offered a theory of organic connection at the level of theme or personal manifestation. Attention invariably focused on the darksome tale of historic guilt and sorrow, which was, in the words of Whipple, "prefaced by some fifty pages of autobiographical matter." No one said so explicitly, but all seemed to sense that the issues of Hester and Dimmesdale were somewhat more complex – or at least more sensitive – than those of Hawthorne and politics. And although these earliest *Scarlet Letter* critics came to disagree most sharply about the moral tendency of the tale "itself," everyone admitted the hypnotic fascination of both its theme and its style.

The very first reviews were, morally speaking, all quite friendly and supportive. Evidently sensing that Hawthorne had taken up a dangerous question, and also (perhaps) that he had treated it in terms more powerful than plain, they hastened to defend in advance the "purity" of his mind and motive. Particularly worried that Hawthorne's moral was "shadowed forth rather than expressed," Ripley quoted a whole long paragraph (on the rationale of Hester's eventual return to New England) to point up that moral for all those not "wise enough to detect it." Evert Duyckinck strenuously insisted that the lesson was "severe" but "wholesome," and indeed more salutary than anything one was likely to hear "from the degenerate successors of Cotton Mather." And Whipple, elaborating Duyckinck's praise of Hawthorne's unique ability to handle his "delicate subject without an infusion of George Sand," loudly protested that "the most abandoned libertine could not read the volume without being thrilled into something like virtuous resolution." Lurking here, quite plainly, is the suspicion that someone might read the book seeking thrills of different kind; or else, more generally, that successfully dramatized works of fiction have the power to move readers well beyond, and possibly in spite of, the limits of any moral language officially provided. So that what we get, from these friendliest of reviewers, is a slightly anxious assurance that we may safely trust, in the end, both the *teller* and the *tale* of *The Scarlet Letter*.

Yet the reaction – in moral terms, at least – was not long in coming. No fewer than three original reviews insisted that Hawthorne's new departure in fiction was indeed undermoralized, and that its tendencies were by no means uniformly wholesome. Most famously (and most hysterically, as we now regard the issues), an Episcopal bishop named Arthur Cleveland Coxe rebuked Hawthorne for ignoring a wealth of more suitable "historical" matters in favor of "the nauseous amour of a Puritan pastor" and railed that, in Hawthorne's tale, a "lady's frailty is philosophized into a natural and necessary result of the Scriptural law of marriage." Others tried to make a similar religious point a little more soberly. Acknowledging Hawthorne's work as one of "rare [and] we may say of fearful power," Orestes Brownson pointed to the decidedly "unmoral" character of much of the characters' sufferings and accused Hawthorne of subscribing to the "modern doctrine that represents the affections as fatal" — which is to say that the categories of *The Scarlet Letter* are at bottom more "naturalistic" than Christian. And Anne Abbott, who had anticipated Brownson's own formulations, inserted a protest against the power of fiction itself: "devils and angels are alike beautiful, when seen through the magic glass."

Hysteria subsides. Yet the orthodox reviewers of *The Scarlet Letter* may have noticed something: Moral questions in Hawthorne's fiction must be handled with care; and as for moral prescriptions, shake well before using. We may not *yet* understand the precise mixture of moralism and social science expressed in the narrative voice that (re-)tells the story of Hester Prynne. And it would be folly to suppose that critics will soon say the last word on either sex or Puritanism.

Something like this latter point is pursued — at length, and to some fair purpose — by what may strike us as the most "modern" of the original reviewers of *The Scarlet Letter*. Where others had thought chiefly to praise and blame Hawthorne's own morality, George Bailey Loring attempted to get inside the logic of the characters themselves, and in a way we can think of as significantly "historical." To be sure, Hawthorne was *himself* regularly associated with the Puritanism of his sources; there, it was supposed, lay the springs of terror in his peculiar form of "psychological romance." And Coxe went so far as to concede that Hawthorne's historical "scene-painting is in a great degree true to a period of our Colonial history"; but he hastened to wish that the portrait had been more "patriotic." And then even this attenuated form of historical interest was swamped by his overflowing concern for present sexual mores. So that Loring's response indeed stands out as the most "objective" analysis of the significance of moral experience within a plausible imitation of an actual past. For Loring, Hester and Dimmesdale feel, act, and suffer not precisely as we might morally prefer but about as we might historically expect.

Anxious to validate and uphold the dogmatic proposition that "the sanctity of the devoted relation between the sexes has [indeed] constituted the most certain foundation of all purity and all social safety," Loring nevertheless regards the problem of Puritanism as a failure to recognize "the intention or meaning of [the] sensuous element in human nature." Even more startlingly, he seriously invites us to imagine "the consternation and disgust which overwhelmed our forefathers when the majesty of virtue, and the still mightier majesty of the law, were affronted." Fully alert to the untoward social consequences of the "wayward act of passion," and quite prepared to grant that "the safety of associated man demands all the compromises which the superficiality of the social law creates," Loring yet sees the modernity and power of *The Scarlet Letter* in its sympathetic, "inside" portrayal of the well nigh inevitable clash between the social and the passional:

> We see in the lives of Arthur Dimmesdale and Hester Prynne, that the severity of puritanic law and morals could not keep them from violation; and we see, too, that this very severity drove them both into a state of moral insanity. And does any benefit arise from such a sacrifice?

Evidently, the problem of *The Scarlet Letter* goes deeper – and extends further back – than could be allowed by those who feared, with Bishop Coxe, that Hawthorne had merely begun the lascivious "French era" in our literature. Apparently it was a sign of more than Hawthorne's own repressed, "Victorian" times.

3

"Modern" criticism of *The Scarlet Letter* (however one chooses to determine the beginning of that problematic phase) can scarcely be said to have solved either the abstract moral or the concrete historical problem that richly evocative text forces on every reader: Considered "then" or considered "now," what does this story of "passion and authority" manage to signify? Probably no two readers would agree on the net accomplishment of all those books and articles that run – intermittently at first, and then, with the establishment of academic criticism, more or less continuously – from Henry James's *Hawthorne* (1879) to the most recent efforts in our proliferated array of scholarly journals. But probably it would be only a little unfair to say that Hawthorne's art has counted for more than his moral vision.

Not that the latter has been ignored, powerful and insistent as it is. Yet the literary sophistication of what we still call the "New Criticism" involved a clearsighted and cautious appreciation of the complex delicacy with which any fiction achieves its thematic resolution and a strong sense that Hawthorne's fictions count among the *most* complex and delicate we know. Further, the insights of psychoanalysis have suggested that, as human motivations may be inherently ambivalent, so our deepest expressions may be significantly ambiguous; and that there is no reason to suppose Hawthorne was any more singleminded than anyone else. Thus, as professional interpreters learned to be as attentive to the implications of imagery, structure, and narrative strategy as ordinary readers have always been to the explicit pronouncements of moral rhetoric, critical notice has often shifted from the dogmatic *what* to the tentative *how* of Hawthorne's first extended fiction. And surely it will surprise only the very inexperienced reader to learn that the *newest* criticism, carried out under the sign of the "theory of signs," has insisted, most philosophically, on the "indeterminacy" of all verbal meaning. So that interpreting *The Scarlet Letter* may become as risky a project as trying to assign one final significance to the letter with which official Puritanism once thought to sign the moral identity of Hester Prynne herself. And that Hawthorne himself may have known much or all of this in advance.

A brief review must serve – quite selective and self-consciously partial, and all based on the presumption that the serious student of Hawthorne must someday prepare his or her own equally "secondary" list of "original" precursors.[4]

Henry James is usually set down as the first utterly serious critic of "the novel" considered not as popular entertainment but as a first-rate form of literary art. And probably it is equally fair to name him the father of the formalist criticism of Hawthorne's fiction, especially of his "Three American Novels." Taking Hawthorne's morality entirely for granted, and setting himself against a growing tradition of critical emphasis on Hawthorne's own somber neo-Puritanism, James meditates almost exclusively on how *The Scarlet Letter* makes its peculiar artistic impression on the reader. And some of these methods he finds peculiar indeed.

Clearly, James wishes to *posit* the world-class greatness of *The*

Scarlet Letter. The "finest piece of imaginative writing yet put forth in the country," it was as well "a novel that belonged to literature, and to the forefront of it." And yet there is about it, to James's own developing tastes (and, we may fear, competitive instincts), something a bit *too* imaginative, in the weak or merely "fanciful" sense of that word. Denying that its fable was at all a " 'love-story' " and slighting its "so-called historical cast," James reduces Hester to the role of an "accessory" and concentrates on the "cold, thin" light the novel casts on Dimmesdale, upon whom "the *denouement* depends." As he reads it, "The story goes on, for the most part, between the lover and the husband."

An admittedly disproportionate attempt to estimate "the faults of the book" leads to an extended comparison with "the story of *Adam Blair*, by John Gibson Lockhart"; and although James insists that Lockhart's achievement is of a lower order than Hawthorne's, he pretty clearly prefers its warmth and "vulgar" naturalness to the "cold and ingenious fantasy," the "elaborate imaginative delicacy" of Hawthorne's own putative masterpiece. James tries very hard, alternatively, to correct or blame his own responses, but deep down his sense of novelistic realism is offended by conceits such as the "mystic A" burned into Dimmesdale's breast. Thus he presses on with an elaborate specification of *The Scarlet Letter*'s excess of "mechanical" symbolism and ends by sharply blaming Hawthorne's "extreme predilection for a small number of vague ideas . . . represented by such terms as 'sphere' and 'sympathies.' " In fact, therefore, the premise of Hawthorne's world-class artistry, conceded at the outset, is strongly challenged in the outcome.

With friends like James, one might suppose, Hawthorne's modern reputation would scarcely require any enemies. Yet severe critics there have been, and most if not all appear to take inspiration from James's fairly harsh strictures on Hawthorne's literary grasp of reality. The story is too long (and too complicated) to be rehearsed in an essay such as this one, but the scholar of *The Scarlet Letter* must eventually notice that critics as important (and diverse) as William Crary Brownell, Van Wyck Brooks, Vernon L. Parrington, and, moving closer to our own "golden age" of Hawthorne criticism, Marius Bewley, Martin Green, and (on occasion) Lionel Trilling can all sound the Jamesean note of "reality" as opposed to a somewhat too curious exercise of the metaphysical fancy.[5] Hawthorne's imaginative world, all these distinguished observers seem to suspect, is filled with arcane or magic signs, which insist on themselves as such but which do not point to anything truly worthy of our own substantial notice.

On the other hand, however, the friendliest of Hawthorne's explicit enemies aroused suspicions somewhat more pregnant of sophisticated critical possibility. Where James may have been *silently* trying to write himself out of an undue reverence for his most celebrated American precursor, D. H. Lawrence is *avowedly* intent on exposing and hence placing himself, once and for all, beyond all the pious delusions he once absorbed from the stated premises of "classics" of American literature – including, preeminently perhaps, the various morals of *The Scarlet Letter*. Because Lawrence is arguing, all at once, a great variety of personal and public cases, his essay is almost impossible to summarize; students still find it both provocative and maddening. Yet "Nathaniel Hawthorne and *The Scarlet Letter*" constitutes the crucial chapter in Lawrence's *Studies in Classic American Literature* (1923) and remains an important landmark in the modern criticism of Hawthorne's essential text.

What Lawrence intuits, most fundamentally, is that Hester Prynne is indeed at the center of *something* in *The Scarlet Letter*, that she animates a certain subversive protest that Hawthorne's "romance" (here specifically so called)[6] effectively registers. Truly the denouement depends on the last-moment confession of Dimmesdale, and thus he indeed dominates the book's rational structure, even as James had observed. But the emotional texture is all Hester, and her stubborn insistence on the "consecration" of her unreconstructed sexuality somehow gives the lie to everything else. Dimmesdale appears to die of his sin, and he goes to judgment with as clear a conscience as Puritan logic knew how to arrange. But Hester "lives." The narrator distrusts her logic and fears for her soul but, deeper down, the text stands fairly in awe of her simple power: "Woman is the nemesis of doubting man. She can't help it."

Clearly, more is at issue than the morality questioned by the early reviewers – the complex fact that Hester is neither fully repentant of her sin nor adequately punished by God. Firmly convinced that "sin" is but "the breaking of one's own integrity," Lawrence is obviously in no position to criticize a novelist's refusal to mystify the Christian sexual ethic. But it is also clear that Lawrence regards the problem of Hawthorne's "art" in distinctly non–Jamesian terms. Although a considerable artist in the novel form, Lawrence is less a worshiper of mimetic propriety than a prophet of the quietly subversive power of all "art-speech." What he wishes to assert is not only that fictions have an extraordinary power to form belief and motivate choice, but also, more radically, that the makers of fiction are not always in a position to control (or even always to grasp) the range of motives they release into these elaborate fictional constructs. Thus the springs of literary power – so keenly sensed by *all* the early reviewers – may have little enough to do with either mimetic decorum or properly pointed morals. The heart has its own reasons; and, further, all signs are signs of *something*.

Disturbing as they are, Lawrence's suggestions did not immediately find their way into the critical (now academic) mainstream. But they did eventually, and little by little their effect has been revolutionary. As a result, a number of well-made cases now seem a little old-fashioned: Austin Warren strenuously asserts the orthodoxy of Hawthorne's "Calvinism" (*Nathaniel Hawthorne,* 1938); Yvor Winters magisterially defends the integrity of a puritanic "allegory" turned somehow "against the Puritans themselves" (*Maule's Curse,* 1934); and F. O. Matthiessen carefully explains that Hawthorne's "variety of symbolic reference," epitomized by the "device of multiple choice," can be called "allegory" only in defiance of the authority of Coleridge (*American Renaissance,* 1941). Important clarifications occur, but each of these claims is noticeably lacking in Lawrence's "modern" sense that there is something self-contradictory about Hawthorne's masterpiece, and that it gains rather than loses interest by an all-out pursuit of its "perfect duplicity."

Much of the specifically "formalist" criticism of *The Scarlet Letter* also lacks this sense. Or fails to emphasize it, at least, and so may strike present-day readers as rendering Hawthorne's unsettling performance a little too rationally schematic to be quite true. Em-

14

phasizing Hawthorne's "fine-art devices in fiction," Leland Schubert justly observes that the "pattern" of Hawthorne's story appears "clear and beautiful" as soon as we notice that it is "built around the scaffold," three appearances of which mark a beginning, a middle, and an end (*Hawthorne, the Artist*, 1944). Less classic but equally cogent is John Gerber's insistence on a "four-part form," in which first the Puritan community (Chapters 1–8) and then Chillingworth (9–12), Hester (13–20), and Dimmesdale (21–24) successively precipitate and propel the dramatic action (*New England Quarterly*, 1944). And Malcolm Cowley, as if to complete a needful sequence, makes the case for a "five-act structure" (in Charles Shapiro, ed., *Twelve Original Essays on Great American Novels*, 1958). Each of these discrete claims can seem true enough in its own terms, but all may serve chiefly to remind the reader that when he was *reading* he wasn't really *counting*, that the power of Hawthorne's "form" lies elsewhere.

Even those important ("New") critics whose sense of form has been, famously, far more "organic" than "mechanical" (or even architectonic) convey the impression that the greatness of *The Scarlet Letter* must finally be a function of an effective closure of meaning – however complex or dialectical the process of its evolution. In the midst of an argument that stresses the countervailing significance of "the light and the dark" in Hawthorne's fiction, Richard Harter Fogle concedes that the moral problem that authorizes the "sustained and rigorous dramatic irony" of *The Scarlet Letter* can be solved "only by introducing the supernatural level of heaven," somewhere beyond the humane complement of "head and heart"; but he seems entirely comfortable in evoking it, critically, as an absence whose virtual presence effectively redeems all other signs of a hopeless "ambiguity of moral meaning" (*Hawthorne's Fiction*, 1952). Thinking more naturalistically, Roy Male contends that Hawthorne's narrative never loses sight of its originary symbolic contrast "between the wild rose and the prison door." But if the former, which is organic, finally defeats the latter, which is mechanical, the effect is merely to "complement and intensify" Hawthorne's universal theme of "the entangled good and evil in human life" (ELH, 1953). And even Hyatt Waggoner's most subtle literary calculus of symbolic cemetery, prison, and rose – itself informed by a clear sense that these symbols exist for persons who "have histories and are involved in the larger movements of history" — may well imply a final resolution of all natural and moral ambiguity at the level of Hawthorne's perfect art.

Much different is the impression created by one of the most felicitously titled articles ever written about Hawthorne — "Scarlet A Minus" by Frederick I. Carpenter, which appeared in *College English* for 1944. Insisting that the art of *The Scarlet Letter* is in fact "less than perfect," Carpenter yet pursues the odd (Lawrentian) argument that its "very imperfection . . . makes it classic." The problem, as Carpenter formulates it, is that the drama of Hawthorne's text actually supports three separate answers — yes, no, and partly — to the thematically unavoidable question of the "sinfulness" of the "action symbolized by the scarlet letter"; and his final contention is that Hawthorne has "imposed a moralistic 'Conclusion' upon the drama which his characters had enacted." Or else, more generally, that Hawthorne's "moralistic passages never remotely admitted the possible truth of the . . . ideal which he had objectively described Hester Prynne as realizing."

Carpenter cites Lawrence only as an (ambiguous) exponent of the "gospel of love" school, but the connection seems stronger than that. Their essential agreement is on the strength and centrality of the character of Hester and, even more fundamentally, on the novel's inability or unwillingness to say out loud all that might be said for Hester's line of thought and action. Perfectly recapitulated, in fact, and much more patiently spelled out, is Lawrence's premise that Hawthorne's "tale" and his "teller" are not always telling us the same thing.

What might be expected to follow from some such insight, logically, is a strenuous analysis of the narrative technique of *The Scarlet Letter*, perhaps even the identification of some narrative "persona" by which to characterize the partial or, at all events peculiar, sorts of moral rhetoric the work in fact contains, certainly in relation to the highly stylized *self*-characterization Hawthorne provides in "The Custom-House." But although that curious preface has indeed become the subject of some fairly searching modern analyses (generating a separate history too complex to be attempted here), it has not usually been approached in just that way.

Nor has the "narrator" of *The Scarlet Letter* become, until quite recently, a subject of separate critical investigation.[7] Evidently the self-contradictions of the narrative "itself" have presented a problem that, once apprehended, has proved hard to get beyond.

Thus a number of articles (not specifically mentioned here) try to get Hester just right — either to harmonize her subversive appeal with the suggestions of authorial rhetoric or else to show just where and how far she exceeds the mark. That problem is still worth considering. So is the question of Pearl as a symbolic indicator, wavering or stable, of the novel's moral center, allegorical or otherwise. So also is Hester's evident competition with Dimmesdale to have the book's last word: his (possibly reconverted) emphasis on "the law we broke" versus her (not entirely resubmissive) vision of a "new truth [to be] revealed." And so, finally, is *someone's* attempt to plot "the dark problem of this life" along an axis of historical progress. All of these enduring interests clearly suggest that the primary human or thematic appeal of *The Scarlet Letter* continues to make it difficult for all but the most determined critical readers to isolate its art as such[8] — as if the chief effect of that art had been to portray a problem that *no one* connected with the story is in any position to solve.

Some such insight appears to be the moral of Ernest Sandeen's excellent study of "*The Scarlet Letter* as a Love Story" (PMLA, 1962), which suggests that the "mystery" of this "haunted book" is as much that of "erotic passion" as of "sin," and proceeds to show how many of the novel's motivational cruxes can be solved by the simple observation that neither Hester nor Dimmesdale can quite get past the fact that they passionately love each other. A similar perception governs Seymour Gross's penetrating analysis of the "conflict of moralities" that necessarily results from the fact that, although Hester Prynne possesses ample "integrity in her own terms," she has nevertheless "fallen in love with a minister who has integrity in different terms"; so that, whatever we decide about "the right" of the matter, what counts most is the final, "tragic" fact "that Dimmesdale is dead and Hester is alone" (*CLA Journal*, 1968). And it clearly informs Charles Feidelson's most subtle combination of symbolic and social analysis, which stresses the way all "the Puritans of *The Scarlet Letter* are deeply involved in the dialectic of modern freedom" – from which Hawthorne, given his "historical method," has neither the "right" nor the "desire" to rescue them (in R. H. Pearce, ed., *Hawthorne Centenary Essays,* 1964). No less a critic than Austin Warren might dissent from this growing consensus – that self-contradiction is of the essence of the material Hawthorne dared to investigate. But although his "casuistic" analysis of the difference between "penance" and "penitence" remains classic, few modern critics agree that we should read *The Scarlet Letter* as a powerfully self-coherent "Literary Exercise in Moral Theology" (*Southern Review,* 1965). Most give the impression, rather, that it quite baffles most of the available categories.

Yet of the making of categories there is – to paraphrase Ecclesiastes – no end. And the powerful ones of Freud have been skillfully brought to bear on *The Scarlet Letter* by Frederick Crews, whose *Sins of the Fathers* (1966) may be thought of as elevating (or reducing) the not always coherent suggestions of D. H. Lawrence, himself a notable reader of Freud, to the level of psychological science. Often concerned with turning Freud's "terrible certainty" that "the ego is not master in its own house" against the rhetorical ambiguities of Hawthorne's own art, Crews focuses here, in a chapter called "The Ruined Wall," on the abundant self-conflict of Dimmesdale's moral career: What Warren (and the narrative) call "penance" stands clearly forth as a masochistic symptom that "Dimmesdale shows the neurotic's reluctance to give up."

Taking entirely for granted Lawrence's premise that we are naive to trust the pious rhetoric of Hawthorne's "teller," Crews clearly suggests that the true interest of *The Scarlet Letter* must attach to its virtually clinical portrayal of Dimmesdale's unwonted surrender to "libidinal impulse." In these terms, it appears that fleshly pain and fleshly pleasure are even more alike than are, in the narrator's final formula, "hatred and love." Accordingly, we notice that, since Dimmesdale is unwilling to admit that "his libidinous wishes are really his," all his mental energy is directed toward "repressing" them in so manifestly physical a way that the libido can "gratify itself surreptitiously." Subsequently, Dimmesdale's not quite hearty decision to flee with Hester succeeds only in doubling the "opposing force of [repressive] conscience, which will be stronger in proportion to the libidinal threat." So that, ultimately, Dimmesdale's behavior in the final scaffold scene represents merely "the conclusion to the breakdown of repression." Counterbalancing this story, we have only "the case of Hester," whose "penitence seems to be devoid of theological content," returning to Boston because it offers her " 'a more real life' than she could find elsewhere, even with Pearl." Thus, apparently, will moral ambiguity always submit to the clarifications of psychoanalytic analysis.

Yet other modern systems do not sponsor quite so clear and scientific a resolution of human conflict into deep structure. Certainly feminism does not, commited as it is to the belief that adequate psychological depth does not preclude an appropriate ethical or political circumspection. Accordingly, Nina Baym proposes – systematically, if serially – that *The Scarlet Letter* reveals Hawthorne's complex involvement in what we have come to call "sexual politics." In her view, Hawthorne presents Dimmesdale as a young man too powerfully invested in conserving the world of Puritan "patriarchs," and that "he holds this position by a kind of resolute clinging to childhood." Hester, by sympathetic contrast, is revealed as deeply radical. Her commitment to Pearl, to the "art" of her needlework, and to innovative speculation all testify to some "ultimately unshakeable belief in the goodness" of her private, female nature – which alone saves her from the ultimate sin of witchcraft (*New England Quarterly*, 1970). This dramatic contrast, Baym further argues, is personally adumbrated in Hawthorne's account, in "The Custom-House," of his own divided loyalties (ESQ, 1973). It finally expresses itself as a theory of Hawthorne's Hester-like rebellion against the intense conservatism of his imagined readership (*The Shape of Hawthorne's Career*, 1975).[9]

Baym's Hawthorne is thus plainly a "romantic," if only "*malgré lui*." And although her *Scarlet Letter* is every bit as secular as Crew's, it is less closed off by the analysis of psychological symptoms than it is opened up to debate about persons with political histories. A further sign of such critical reopening may be seen in a recent rich, idiomatically mixed essay by David Leverenz, which emphasizes the problem of "reading" Hawthorne's *Scarlet Letter*, of learning to make our way through (and perhaps live with) its now famous network of "unresolved tensions." Enacting Lawrence's "directive to trust the tale, not the teller," whose moral stance is characterized as "inauthentic," Leverenz yet offers a narrator who "functions less as a character than as a screen for the play of textual energies." And moving through a subtle enough deployment of *both* psychoanalytic and feminist possibilities, touching *both* Hester and Dimmesdale, Leverenz concludes on an altogether unsystematic note: "Hester's life continues to speak with embattled vitality" (*Nineteenth-Century Fiction*, 1983). Life, it appears, can always be affirmed, even when it defies our categories; and *The Scarlet Letter* provides as fair an occasion as most.

Perhaps we ought to let that stand as the last word, or even as the "moral" of some *very* sophisticated modern attempts to subdue the dramatic vitality of Hawthorne's masterwork. Still, we must notice that what Leverenz calls "textual energies" others might prefer to name the "play of language" or even the autonomous "life of the signifier." For in the end *The Scarlet Letter* is, as its own central symbol insists, a linguistic fact as well as a vital sign. Thus its power to prove, over and over again, that it means more than it (or we) can quite *say* is only half the problem; the other half is that the linguistic signs in which its life appears to reside have the power to say more than one person could ever quite *mean*. And to that complex philosophical fact, the appropriate critical response would seem to be not silence but renewed if chastened interpretation.

"Silence" has indeed been proposed, by one recent and fairly strenuous "postmodernist" reading, as the essential condition of meaning in *The Scarlet Letter*—that silence about relationships that denies each of its characters his or her true (relational) identity, and that (much more abstractly) is better overcome by fiction than any other less "merciful" form of writing. So too, just previously, has been a form of Hegel's dialectic of "Spirit," as if to resolve into history the characters' typically romantic search for some stable, transcendental signifier, of self or world. And so, just prior to that, has been a theory of Hawthorne's romance form as a *fiction* of coherence based on a radical discontinuity of elements.[10] Such readings, whether one likes them or not, may fairly be called "metacritical," aiming not at a categorical reformulation of plot or dramatic action but rather at a philosophical identification of the novelist's own array of constructive categories. Their themes are "metathemes," the epistemological power of which turns Hester's passion pale with naive thematic embarrassment. Likely to arise whenever interpreters have lost humanistic or historical interest in an author's religious or philosophical meanings, or when they have begun to doubt the possibility of "re-cognizing" an author's conscious intentions, such efforts provide a way of mastering a text at the highest level of structural or linguistic analysis – while draining it, at the same time, of the very qualities that engage most readers and baffle ordinary critics.

Yet one such metatheme may well survive its own "deconstructive" danger. Not by virtue of its being ultimate, although it would indeed seem to be that, but rather by the fact that it well recapitulates the passionate speculation of everyone involved in and concerned with *The Scarlet Letter*. Well anticipated by every reading that stresses the heuristic or educative value or Hawthorne's own preliminary ("Custom-House") struggle to grasp the significance of a faded letter; fairly announced by discussions which assert that Hawthorne's narrative works to turn "letter into hieroglyph" or which stress its study of "the meaning of meaning";[11] it receives its full, humane, and lucid account in Millicent Bell's essay entitled "The Obliquity of Signs" (*Massachusetts Review*, 1982).

The point is not merely that every character in *The Scarlet Letter* essentially rehearses Hawthorne's own preliminary attempt to assign definitive significance to the letter/symbol **A**. Or even that they and we all try and fail to know the moral "essences" of their and our fellow sinners. It is, rather, that *The Scarlet Letter* may be, quite deliberately, and "as much as any work of fiction can be, an essay in semiology," whose theme is "the obliquity or indeterminacy of signs." It seems quite sound, biographically, to speculate that "Hawthorne may have had similar reasons to our own for questioning – while performing – the interpretation of experience as a species of message." And it overstates the case only slightly to suggest that from this metatheme "derives the peculiar life of those other themes which might otherwise seem lacking in modern interest." Somewhat more empirically: Some readers are no longer interested in the question of "sin"; others may even be a little bored with "art," if not with sex; but who can read *The Scarlet Letter* without *some* self-conscious questioning of his own textually enforced quest for meaning in linguistic symbols? And without realizing, all the while, that this speculative metaquestion is not entirely separate from the text's own most primitive inquisitions? For how *do* we pursue its signs of life apart from the life of signs?

4

The reader must not suppose – in delight or in terror – that the essays in the present volume have been selected and arranged to adumbrate or to contest the precise present state of categorical metacriticism – or indeed to illustrate any ideal division or conflict of theory or "approach." Rather, and much more simply, the contributions represent nothing more than the result of an (editorial) guess about *persons* who might have something fresh and useful to say about a text with a critical history far less neatly simplified than the foregoing remarks have managed to suggest. There is no single, agreed-upon point of critical departure. And each essay must make clear its own necessary precursors.

Yet it seems only fair to remark that, in fact, each of the essays in this volume is significantly "historical" in its approach to Hawthorne's much disputed text; and that the total impression they make is noticeably more "historicist" than the established body of thematic or formal criticism. *Not* that they all try to account for Hawthorne's relation to (or use of) his Puritan materials or attend to his techniques as an "historical novelist." The scope is considerably broader than that, as each of the contributors imagines the being or pertinence of history in a different way. The common loyalty appears only in a certain shared sense that there are things to know – about various contexts in which *The Scarlet Letter* may be viewed, or about traditions in which it appears to participate – which can make a meaningful difference to the modern reader's response. Evidently more than "background studies," all of the essays finally come to rest in a "reading" of the text. Each claims to discover something "within" the work itself, even if this "something" is only a marked variation or striking absence.

Furthermore, these "contextual" readings are, all of them, self-consciously "plural": none means to cancel out any other; nor does their composite in any sense exhaust the approaches which special knowledge may suggest. None pretends to be "final," even in its own order of explanation. Serviceable rather than imperialist, each tries merely to suggest that apt learning, judiciously applied, may advance rather than close off commentary. Or else – to risk at once the grandest claim of the historical critic – that some reference to the realm of plural yet not altogether arbitrary context may serve to delimit an otherwise boundless domain of available misprision.

Thus Michael Bell has thought to argue that some awareness of the conventions (and even of the epistemology) of the "romance" will prevent a naive response to much that is "said" in *The Scarlet Letter*, including its suitably admonitory and even proto-thematic "Custom-House" preface. Originally understood as an essentially subversive or revolutionary mode of writing, romance must be recovered as essentially an "art of deception," overtly reassuring while, deeper down, it works to unsettle or embarrass the shape of custom and belief. If "novel" exists to tell the story of available truth, "romance" keeps reminding us, subtly, that there are holes in that story. Hence Bell's emphasis on omission, indirection, and near-contradiction in an apparently ingenuous introduction leads on to a discussion of a plot which raises the problem of truth versus deception (including self-deception) to a condition of human being. And hence the plausibility of his most paradoxical conclusion, that the most famous of the "many morals" of *The Scarlet Letter* – "Be true! Be true! Be true!" – may be a moral saying that all but unsays itself, appropriately, in a form of fiction which owes its existence and continuing vitality to the philosophic suspicion that no such wisdom can ever enact itself in human language.

Perhaps some readers will find that too radical a skepticism to cover the whole of Hawthorne's curious mixture of piety and radicalism. Yet there is no evading the practical consequence of Bell's more preliminary suggestion that romance means to be "more fictional" than other fictional modes – namely, that its thematic resolutions will be proportionately more difficult to decipher and arrange. Intellectual closure, if there is to be any at all, will surely occur in terms other than those most comfortably provided. And probably some such insight motivates the complex investigations of David Van Leer, for whom intellectual redundancy and even the appearance of stylistic incoherence threaten all moral repose from the outset.

Attending to questions of "discourse" rather than "genre," Van Leer points out a certain tension between Hawthorne's ostensible Puritan setting and his noticeably romantic language: Events ascribed to a fiction of the seventeenth century are repeatedly "explicated" in an idiom more proper to Emerson than to John Cotton. Evidently some intellectual "translation" is occurring, even as someone tries to get to the heart of a matter at once historical and elementary or universal. What this suggests, first of all, is the presence of a "narrator," a fictional voice sufficiently distinct from "Hawthorne himself" that his authority to pronounce on "the meaning" of events cannot be taken at face value. And ultimately, of course, it points to the metatheme of the subjectivity of all interpretation as such. Yet Van Leer has another, equally subtle and more contextual point as well. Convinced that the particular *kind* of translation matters as much as the general *fact*, Van Leer persuasively argues that the narrator's standard of "sympathy," which the characters are variously said to respect or violate, is less a wholesome truism than an important clue to a long but dubious tradition of making mental "substances" out of the crucial terms psychic and ethical discourse. So that Hawthorne's intention in *The Scarlet Letter* may be a good deal more revisionist – and more philosophical – than we have ever been willing to allow.

Equally revisionist, though more conventionally historical, are the claims of this editor's own essay, on the potent reality and the equally powerful metaphor of sexuality in a tale of unruly love in an ideally lawful Puritan "utopia." Building on various "source studies" and also on my own and other earlier work on Hawthorne's deep involvement in "the matter of the Puritans," I argue (generally) for Hawthorne's vital engagement with the theological politics of John Winthrop's seminal *History of New England* and (specifically) for his shrewdly critical view of the "significance" of Puritan sexual language.[12] So considered, the matter of *The Scarlet Letter* appears not as a moralistic reflection on the consequences of "sin" in the Puritan sense, or even as a psychological analysis of "guilt" in either the Freudian or the supposedly universal sense, but rather as a speculative probing of the power of sexual figures to structure religious ideology and confuse natural experience. Yet the point, it should be noted, is not at all to make Hawthorne's themes "transcend" their local setting. It is, rather, to grasp the extent to which *The Scarlet Letter* strategically epitomizes an entire context of Puritan thought.

Then, finally, as if to reassert that contexts are indeed plural, Carol Bensick returns the reader to certain broader terms of (generic) reference. Responding to the recent identification, by "Europeanists," of a fictional genre that can fairly be called "the novel of adultery," Bensick studies the striking similarities – and also the definitive differences – between *The Scarlet Letter* and other examples of its international kind. Because she treats genre as itself an historical (and not a Platonic) principle, she is able to argue that not only the cultural significance but even the dramatic meaning of the sexual experience of Hester Prynne depends on the terms of a venerable and ongoing tradition of adulterous fictions as crucially as on any other. And what she argues, most arrestingly, is that the survivability of Hester Prynne argues for a "demystified" (even a naturalistic) understanding of the problem of marriage, adultery, and divorce that may embarrass the sexual sociology of so commanding a figure as Tolstoy. She even manages to throw some new light on the deeper meaning of the moralistic protest of Hawthorne's orthodox reviewers.

Whether everything asserted in this volume of essays is perfectly consistent with everything else, the reader of course must judge. So too with the more difficult question of whether their assorted "contextualisms" actually succeed either in narrowing the margin of interpretative irrelevance or in forestalling the advance of skeptical abstraction. But the intention at least should be clear: to enter into what we may still call the "spirit" in which Hawthorne once constructed his romance of sin and of signs – not biographically, to be sure, and certainly not through the white magic of psychoanalytic acumen. But to enter this spirit merely historically – by studying the various word-worlds in which his signs have life. An altogether modest spiritual exercise, by the standards of Dimmesdale or of deconstruction. Yet testing enough for the ongoing life of Hester and of criticism.

NOTES

1 For a more detailed account of Hawthorne's life and career up to and surrounding the publication of *The Scarlet Letter*, the reader is urged to consult one or more of the following studies: Nina Baym, *The Shape of Hawthorne's Career* (Ithaca, N.Y.: Cornell University Press, 1975); James R. Mellow, *Nathaniel Hawthorne in His Own Times* (Boston: Houghton Mifflin, 1980); Arlin Turner, *Nathaniel Hawthorne: A Biography* (New York: Oxford University Press, 1980).

2 Melville's widely reprinted review of Hawthorne's *Mosses from an Old Manse* originally appeared in *The Literary World* 17 (August 24, 1850). It may be conveniently consulted in the Norton Critical Edition of Melville's *Moby-Dick* (New York: Norton, 1967).

3 For a generous gathering of original reviews of *The Scarlet Letter*, see J. Donald Crowley, ed., *Hawthorne: The Critical Heritage* (London: Routledge and Kegan Paul, 1970). All present citations are taken from that source; but see also B. Bernard Cohen, *The Recognition of Nathaniel Hawthorne* (Ann Arbor: University of Michigan Press, 1969).

4 A number of resources (beyond those listed in note 3) are available to assist students in constructing their own histories of *Scarlet Letter* criticism. An evaluative summary of Hawthorne's overall critical history is contained in James Woodress, ed., *Eight American Authors* (New York: Norton, 1971); and this history may be further traced by consulting the successive volumes of *American Literary Scholarship: An Annual*, published annually by Duke University Press, and presently edited by J. Albert Robbins. Many anthologized collections of individual essays and book chapters are also available. Among the most useful are the following: Seymour L. Gross, ed., *A Scarlet Letter Handbook* (San Francisco: Wadsworth, 1960); John C. Gerber, ed., *Twentieth Century Interpretations of The Scarlet Letter* (Englewood Cliffs, N.J.: Prentice Hall, 1968); Arlin Turner, *The Merrill Studies in The Scarlet Letter* (Charles E. Merrill Publishing Co., 1970); and especially the Norton Critical Edition of *The Scarlet Letter* (New York: Norton, 1978).

5 For further elaboration of the "Jamesian" premise, see William Crary Brownell, *American Prose Masters* (New York: Scribner, 1909); Van Wyck Brooks, *America's Coming of Age* (New York: B. W. Heubsch, 1915); Vernon L. Parrington, *Main Currents in American Thought* (New York: Harcourt, Brace, 1927); Marius Bewley, *The Eccentric Design*

(New York: Columbia University Press, 1959); Martin Green, *Re-Appraisals* (New York: Norton, 1963); and Lionel Trilling, "Our Hawthorne," in R. H. Pearce, ed., *Hawthorne Centenary Essays* (Columbus: Ohio State University Press, 1964).

6 For a brief review of the scholars and issues in the novel/romance controversy, see the essay of Michael Bell in this volume, especially the material in his footnote 7.

7 For the materials necessary to reconstruct the (often interwoven) arguments about the significance of "The Custom-House" and the presence of a "narrator" in *The Scarlet Letter*, see the essay of David Van Leer in this volume, especially the sources in his footnote 17.

8 Typical of the more conservative attempts to "compose" the morality of *The Scarlet Letter* might be the following: Darrel Abel, "Hawthorne's Hester," *College English* 13 (1952): 303–309, and "Hawthorne's Dimmesdale: Fugitive from Wrath," *Nineteenth-Century Fiction* 11 (1956): 81–105; Hugh H. Maclean, "Hawthorne's *The Scarlet Letter:* The Dark Problem of This Life," *American Literature* 27 (1955): 12–24; Anne Marie McNamara, "The Character of Flame: The Function of Pearl in *The Scarlet Letter,*" *American Literature* 27 (1956): 537–553; and Edward H. Davidson, "Dimmesdale's Fall," *New England Quarterly* 36 (1963): 358–370.

9 For useful summation of Baym's complex "moderate feminist" position, see her "Introduction" to the Penguin American Library edition of *The Scarlet Letter* (New York: Penguin Books, 1983).

10 The "post-modernist" readings in question are, respectively, Michael Ragussis, "Family Discourse and Fiction in *The Scarlet Letter,*" *ELH* 49 (1982): 863–888; John Carlos Rowe, "The Internal Conflict of Romantic Narrative," *Modern Language Notes* 95 (1980): 1203–1231; and Kenneth Dauber, *Rediscovering Hawthorne* (Princeton, N.J.: Princeton University Press, 1977).

11 For the evolution of the metatheme of "meaning," see Charles R. Feidelson, "*The Scarlet Letter,*" in R. H. Pearce, ed., *Hawthorne Centenary Essays* (Columbus: Ohio State University Press, 1964), pp. 31–77; Gabriel Josipovici, *The World and the Book* (Stanford, Ca.: Stanford University Press, 1971), pp. 155–178; and R. Reed Sanderlin, "Hawthorne's *Scarlet Letter*: A Study in the Meaning of Meaning," *Southern Humanities Review* 9 (1975): 145–157.

12 For the important source studies and also some more thematic investigations of Puritan materials in *The Scarlet Letter*, see footnotes 1–3 of my own essay. For other significant historical criticism, see John E. Becker, *Hawthorne's Historical Allegory* (Port Washington, N.Y.: Ken-

nikat Press, 1971), pp. 88–154; Mukhtar Ali Isani, "Hawthorne and the Branding of William Prynne," *New England Quarterly* 45 (1972): 182–95; and Frederick H. Newberry, "Tradition and Disinheritance in *The Scarlet Letter*," *ESQ* 23 (1977): 1–26.

2

Arts of Deception: Hawthorne, "Romance," and *The Scarlet Letter*

MICHAEL DAVITT BELL

TO many readers, both distinguished literary critics and high school students forced to read *The Scarlet Letter* as a duty, Hawthorne's fiction has seemed mainly solemnly moral and allegorical: "serious," of course, and important, but for these very reasons – to state the matter bluntly – boring. This vision of Hawthorne set in early, and it was early challenged by Hawthorne's admirer, Herman Melville. "The world," Melville proclaimed in 1850, "is mistaken in this Nathaniel Hawthorne. He himself must often have smiled at its absurd misconception of him." "Where Hawthorne is known," Melville observes, "he seems to be deemed a pleasant writer, with a pleasant style – a sequestered, harmless man, from whom any deep and weighty thing would hardly be anticipated: a man who means no meanings"; but the truth, Melville insists, is that Hawthorne is "immeasurably deeper than the plummet of the mere critic." Many of his stories (Melville was reviewing a collection of tales, *Mosses from an Old Manse*) seem "directly calculated to deceive – egregiously deceive – the superficial skimmer of pages."[1]

This was a perceptive comment, and it has proved prophetic of recent developments in Hawthorne criticism. What Melville saw, or claimed, in 1850 is that the "superficial" Hawthorne (the solemn classic now enshrined in literary history and high school curricula) is in fact a sort of mask, half-covering a different Hawthorne, far more subversive and anarchic, certainly far from having the sort of genteel complacency with which Hawthorne has so often been associated. In the past twenty years or so, we have become more sensitive to this hidden quality in Hawthorne's fiction. We have now come to value the ways in which Hawthorne's overt moralizing and allegorizing seem designed to deceive us, to play with our needs and fears, as "superficial skimmers of pages," in order to insinuate a vision that would seem to have little to do with conventional morality or allegory.[2]

What has been less often recognized is that a similar quality of playfully subversive deception is also characteristic of Hawthorne's *critical* writings: his comments on fiction in his prefaces – notably in "The Custom-House," his preface to *The Scarlet Letter*. Many passages in these prefaces have been quoted, again and again, as straightforward statements of artistic intention; they have even been used to bolster sweeping general theories of the distinctive nature of American fiction. What we need to recognize is the extent to which these very passages, to use Melville's words, seem "directly calculated to deceive – egregiously deceive – the superficial skimmer of pages."

I considered calling this essay "The Scarlet Herring"; taste, happily, intervened, but the title did have a serious point. *Webster's* dictionary defines "red herring" as "a diversion intended to distract attention from the real issue."[3] This is precisely the covert function of many of Hawthorne's best-known statements about fiction, those generalizations about its nature and purpose that have long been taken at face value, and it is time we looked at these statements more closely. We need to drop our "plummets" – to quote Melville again, while recognizing that "plummets" may be a bit ponderous for the enterprise – as deeply as possible. Only then can we understand both the drama and the humor of Hawthorne's apparently "official" pronouncements. Only then can we uncover the deepest connections between the play of these pronouncements and the fiction – between the comments on fiction in "The Custom-House," for instance, and the action of *The Scarlet Letter*.

1

Hawthorne always insisted that he wrote "romances," rather than "novels," and most of the general comments on fiction in his prefaces have to do with defining the nature of romance and the difference between the romance and the novel. In 1850 *The Scarlet Letter* was subtitled *A Romance,* and in the following year, in the preface to *The House of the Seven Gables,* Hawthorne set out, apparently, to define his terms. "When a writer calls his work a Romance," the preface begins, "it need hardly be observed that he wishes to claim a certain latitude, both as to its fashion and material, which he would not have felt himself entitled to assume, had he professed to be writing a Novel." The novelist, Hawthorne explains, is confined to "a very minute fidelity, not merely to the possible, but to the probable and ordinary course of man's experience." The romancer, on the other hand, is free to present "the truth of the human heart . . . under circumstances, to a great extent, of [his] own choosing or creation" (vol. II, p. 4).[4]

For Hawthorne, this is to say, a romance is more *fictional,* and therefore less *realistic* (although the term "realism" was not in use in pre–Civil War America), than a novel. Unlike the novelist, the romancer is not tied to conventional reality ("the probable and ordinary course of man's experience"); he is free to indulge the fantastic and the marvelous. For the rest of his life, apparently in these terms, Hawthorne continued to characterize himself as a romancer and his works as romances. In 1852 the key word appeared in the main title of *The Blithedale Romance,* and in 1860 *The Marble Faun* was subtitled *The Romance of Monte Beni.* Moreover, the prefaces to these two works continue to use the definition of "romance" begun in the "The Custom-House" and the preface to *The House of the Seven Gables.*

Hawthorne's reputation as a fiction writer – unlike Melville's, for instance – endured into the years after the Civil War, into the era we are now accustomed to call the "age of realism." But to such post–Civil War admirers as Henry James and William Dean Howells, his insistence that he wrote romances rather than novels was a significant embarrassment. In the climate of the new realism, Hawthorne's affection for romance could only seem unfortunate and old-fashioned, a matter for apology or condescending explanation.[5] This situation persisted well into the twentieth century, and its persistence had a good deal to do with the solidification of Hawthorne's reputation as serious but somehow irrelevant or outmoded.

31

After World War II, however, things began to change, and quite dramatically. In 1947 Lionel Trilling, in an essay entitled "Manners, Morals, and the Novel," contended that the novel "has never really established itself in America" – where, he argued, the novel has always diverged "from its classic intention which . . . is the investigation of the problem of reality beginning in the social field." "The fact is," he wrote, "that American writers of genius have not turned their minds to society." Trilling, in this essay, was not directly concerned with Hawthorne, but he did turn to Hawthorne's prefaces to support his own general assertions. "Hawthorne was acute," he wrote, "when he insisted that he did not write novels but romances – he thus expressed his awareness of the lack of social texture in his work."[6]

Trilling's argument that America has had a distinct tradition in fiction soon became a critical commonplace; and although Trilling himself, like the post–Civil War realists, mainly deplored the effects of this tradition, the modern critics who followed his lead turned his ideas to the purposes of something like national celebration. In 1957, for instance, in *The American Novel and Its Tradition,* Richard Chase argued that "the tradition of romance is major in the history of the American novel but minor in the history of the English novel," giving us our own distinctive answer to the novelistic "great tradition" in British fiction described by F. R. Leavis. A year earlier, Perry Miller had delivered a series of lectures entitled "The Romance and the Novel," similarly arguing that the tradition of American fiction was distinctive, and was a tradition of romance. At this same time, more traditional literary romance (for instance, in Spenser or in Shakespeare's late plays) was acquiring new prestige, largely as a result of Northrop Frye's influential *Anatomy of Criticism* (1957), and such prestige was not unwelcome to proponents of the formal or generic "Americanness" of American fiction. By 1968, in any case, Joel Porte, in *The Romance in America,* felt confident in simply assuming that ours was a distinctive tradition of romance. "It no longer seems necessary," he wrote on the first page of his study, "to argue for the importance of romance as a nineteenth-century American genre."[7]

Needless to say, this rapid shift in academic critical opinion, this sudden conversion to the belief that romance constitutes a distinct and distinguished tradition in American fiction, produced a comparable shift in critical opinion about Hawthorne's comments on fiction in his prefaces. What had made him seem old-fashioned in the later nineteenth century all at once, in the 1950s and 1960s, made him seem central. Again and again, from the 1950s to the present day (although there has been a growing current of dissent[8]), Hawthorne's prefaces have been brought forward as evidence that American fiction writers – at least before the Civil War – *knew* that they were creating a distinctive fictional tradition, a tradition at once specifically national and nevertheless tied to the august tradition of European romance.

One can hardly help speculating about why American romance, a kind of literary embarrassment up to World War II, suddenly became a matter of national pride and an arena of critical consensus. Perhaps, having emerged from the war as a world power, we had to discover a tradition of our own, and the claims of Hawthorne and some of his contemporaries that they wrote romances rather than novels were too convenient to be ignored. During these same years, it is worth noting, the study of American literature as a distinct subject first gained general acceptance in American colleges and universities.

Whatever it may have been, it seems likely that there was *some* external reason, in the 1950s and 1960s, for the growing consensus about American romance, because the actual arguments presented to support the romance hypothesis were often fraught with problems. Chase, for instance, cites the preface to *The Marble Faun* as evidence of Hawthorne's belief that "romance, rather than the novel, was the predestined form of American narrative." The problem is that this is in fact precisely the opposite of what Hawthorne actually says in his preface – his point being, rather, that it is almost *impossible* to write a romance about America, given its lack of ruins, legends, and the like. This, he explains, is why he has chosen to set *The Marble Faun* in Italy.[9] Now Richard Chase was no "superficial skimmer of pages"; he was an astute reader. That he so blatantly misread what Hawthorne says suggests that he very much wanted Hawthorne to have said something else. And although his misreading is an extreme example, it is in many respects typical of the way proponents of the American romance

33

tradition have used Hawthorne's comments on fiction to support their own arguments.

Taken together, moreover, these critics produce no genuine consensus on what romance is or what it does. One could argue, of course, that romance may combine a number of different forms and impulses, but such an argument simply assumes, as a given, what must first be demonstrated – that there *was* a common tradition in nineteenth-century American fiction that it makes sense to describe as romance. The classic studies of American romance produce no such demonstration. Trilling, for instance, locates the distinctiveness of fictional romance in its lack of what he calls "social texture" or "social reality"; unlike novels, he argues, romances do not deal with social "manners." Chase more or less agrees with Trilling, but he locates the *central* distinction of American romance elsewhere: in its cultivation, as he puts it, of "radical forms of alienation, contradiction, and disorder" – all of which he distinguishes from the sense of reconciliation and order supposedly achieved by the most characteristic English novels. For Miller, to cite one more example, what distinguishes American romance is mainly its supposed concern with the wilderness and the irrational. "Nature with a capital N," he writes, "Nature as meaning both universal human nature and natural landscape," is what romance signified in the first half of the nineteenth century.[10]

The more one reads these critics, even as one profits immensely from their insights into the literature they are describing, the more one comes to feel that they are using the term "romance" not to describe a particular literary form (which is what the term is supposed to do), but as a convenient label for *any* qualities they find typical of American fiction, or even of American life generally. Yet this vagueness and confusion are understandable. It is not just that academic critics after World War II felt compelled to discover a uniquely American tradition in fiction. Even more important, one suspects, is the fact that for their evidence that American fiction writers *meant* to cultivate a kind of fiction different from that of England, they turned to Hawthorne's prefaces;[11] the truth is that Hawthorne's definitions of "romance" are as confusing – and in their own way apparently as insufficient – as the twentieth-century

34

theories that have been based on them. It is thus hardly surprising that literary historians drawing upon Hawthorne's "generic" categories have found themselves in a state of confusion. The problem is not so much that they have misunderstood what Hawthorne was saying as that they have paid insufficient attention to the way he was saying it. Such attention now needs to be paid. We need to reexamine the well-known descriptions of "romance" in Hawthorne's prefaces, not just as statements but as performances.

2

We might take another look, for instance, at Hawthorne's most frequently quoted definition of "romance" in the first paragraph of his preface to *The House of the Seven Gables:*

> When a writer calls his work a Romance, it need hardly be observed that he wishes to claim a certain latitude, both as to its fashion and material, which he would not have felt himself entitled to assume, had he professed to be writing a Novel. The latter form of composition [i.e., the Novel] is presumed to aim at a very minute fidelity, not merely to the possible, but to the probable and ordinary course of man's experience. The former [i.e., the Romance] – while, as a work of art, it must rigidly subject itself to laws, and while it sins unpardonably, so far as it may swerve aside from the truth of the human heart – has fairly a right to present that truth under circumstances, to a great extent, of the writer's own choosing or creation. (Vol. II, p. 1)

The first thing we might note here is a kind of slippery evasiveness. What the writer wishes to claim "need hardly be observed"; what matters is what he would feel himself "entitled to assume"; the writer might have "*professed* to be writing a Novel"; that form "is *presumed* to aim at a very minute fidelity." The key terms here seem to have meaning, not in and of themselves, but only in the context of a process of negotiation or even pretense. What is the difference, one wonders, between *writing* a novel and *professing* to write a novel? Hawthorne's assumption that the novel/romance distinction is so widely accepted as hardly to require explanation is also somewhat disingenuous. As Nina Baym has pointed out, after examining reviews of fiction in American periodicals from 1840 to

35

1860, this distinction was neither very important nor very clear to Hawthorne's contemporaries.[12] Moreover, if the meaning of calling one's work a romance were so clear as hardly to require explanation, one wonders why Hawthorne feels compelled to explain it.

Briefly summarized, what this opening paragraph from the *Seven Gables* preface says is, as I have already noted, that a romance is distinguished by its "latitude," by its freedom from the novel's obligation to "minute fidelity . . . to the probable and ordinary course of man's experience." This is fine as far as it goes, but it does not, in fact, go very far at all. This is a curiously negative definition: It tells us what romance does *not* do, but tells us almost nothing about what it *does*. More importantly, and closely related to this first sort of reticence, the preface says nothing at all about *why* a writer might wish to depart from ordinary, novelistic realism.

My point might be more clearly expressed in slightly different terms. Hawthorne, in the *Seven Gables* preface, clearly identifies what we might call the *authority* of the novelist. The authority behind his fictions – the "truth" of which those fictions are an expression or representation – is the kind of "fact" studied by historians or, in our own time, by psychologists and sociologists: "the probable and ordinary course of man's experience." What the preface does not identify is the authority of the *romancer*. We learn nothing about the distinctive sorts of truth on which the romancer's fictions are based (both the novel and the romance, apparently, deal with "the truth of the human heart"), and this omission is crucial. The romancer presumably writes a different kind of fiction because he is concerned with a different kind or order of truth. What Hawthorne doesn't tell us is what this truth is.

What seems most interesting about the *Seven Gables* preface, then, is what it does *not* say, and it seems likely that Hawthorne's silence here about what romance is – about the sort of truth that authorizes it – is quite deliberate. This silence allows him to conceal the nature of romance even as he seems to explain it, and if this is what Hawthorne was up to, his strategy has proved remarkably successful. Generations of critics have quoted this passage as a straightforward and complete definition of "romance" without noticing how little it actually says. Instead, they have filled in the gap with their own ideas about the distinctive truth of the romancer: the absence of social "reality" for Trilling, alienation and radical disorder for Chase, "Nature with a capital **N**" for Miller.

If Hawthorne wrote the *Seven Gables* preface to conceal, rather than reveal, the true authority behind romance, if he set out here "to deceive – egregiously deceive – the superficial skimmer of pages," he had good reason for doing so. According to conventional opinion in the first half of the nineteenth century, imaginative fiction, as opposed to literature based on fact, was deeply dangerous, psychologically threatening, and even socially subversive. Thomas Jefferson, for instance, wrote of fiction in 1818 that "when this poison infects the mind, it destroys its tone and revolts it against wholesome reading. Reason and fact, plain and unadorned, are rejected. . . . The result is a bloated imagination, sickly judgment, and disgust towards all the real businesses of life." Jefferson may sound a bit hysterical to modern readers (although his warning is strikingly similar to modern alarm about the dangerous effects of television on impressionable viewers), but what he says here is quite typical of early-nineteenth-century American comments on the dangers of fiction; and these attitudes endured, albeit in less virulent forms, into the middle of the century and beyond. To Hawthorne's contemporaries, what I have called the authority of romance, of imaginative fiction as opposed to factual history, was clear, and it was clearly dangerous. Romance, according to conventional opinion, derived from "sickly" imagination rather than from "wholesome" reason or judgment. To indulge in the delusions of romance was to undermine the basis of psychological and social order, to alienate oneself from "the real businesses of life."[13]

The term "romance," at least implicitly, was thus less a neutral generic label than a revolutionary, or at least antisocial, slogan. To identify oneself as a romancer was to reject far more than "the probable and ordinary course course of man's experience"; it was to set oneself in opposition to the most basic norms of society: reason, fact, and "real" business. In 1848 Herman Melville, who would later delight in Hawthorne's deceptions, wrote a letter to his British publisher, John Murray, announcing that his third book, *Mardi,* would be quite different from its more or less factual predecessors, *Typee* and *Omoo*. "My *instinct*," Melville declared, "is to out with the Romance, & let me say that instincts are prophetic, & better than acquired wisdom."[14] To "out with the Romance" was, for Melville, to rebel, to reject the authority of "acquired wisdom" (of reason, fact, and judgment) for the subversive authority of "instinct" and imagination. Melville's publisher understood him perfectly. A conservative purveyor of safely factual narratives, John Murray was not at all pleased by this letter, and when Melville finally finished his romance, Murray refused to publish it.

In this context, the *Seven Gables* preface is a truly remarkable performance. Hawthorne was fascinated with the antisocial and abnormal, but he never openly identified himself with them. Thus, in the preface, Hawthorne, or the persona he adopts, openly announces that his book is a romance; yet this persona manages to seem wholly ignorant, as Hawthorne himself surely was not, of the subversive implications of such an announcement. He makes it sound perfectly safe, straightforward, morally neutral; the "superficial skimmer of pages" would see no reason to be alarmed. Still, the careful reader would notice that although Hawthorne ignores the conventional sense of the subversive authority of romance, he does not specifically reject it, and he puts nothing else in its place.

Melville openly and repeatedly announced his decision to reject "acquired wisdom" for rebellious "instinct," and this is one of the reasons he lost his reading public during the 1850s. As he became more and more open, critics and readers became more and more hostile.[15] Hawthorne was far more circumspect, which is surely one of the reasons why, unlike Melville, he *was* able to keep his reading public. When Hawthorne proclaimed his own decision to "out with the Romance," he was careful, to use Melville's phrase, "to deceive – egregiously deceive – the superficial skimmer of pages." To miss this quality in the *Seven Gables* preface is to fall for the deception.

The same sort of deception is at work in Hawthorne's discussion of fiction in the "Custom-House" preface to *The Scarlet Letter*. "Romance" is there defined, in another often quoted passage, as "a neutral territory, somewhere between the real world and fairyland, where the Actual and Imaginary may meet, and each imbue itself with the nature of the other" (p. 36). This sounds like a pretty safe (hence, "neutral") definition, certainly a far cry from Melville's defiant rejection of fact for fantasy. Romance, as Hawthorne here describes it, seems to *reconcile* fantasy and fact, the "Imaginary" and the "Actual." But there are serious problems lurking in even this celebrated formulation, problems we see clearly if we place the passage in the context of Hawthorne's preface as a whole.

"The Custom-House" is mainly devoted to describing Hawthorne's experience as Surveyor of Customs at Salem from 1846 to 1849. It also tells the story — which Hawthorne, of course, made up — of what he found, one day, in the attic of the Custom-House: a frayed scarlet A, made of cloth, and a manuscript summarizing the life of the woman who wore the letter, one Hester Prynne. We are told that the manuscript was the work of Hawthorne's eighteenth-century predecessor, Surveyor Pue, and we are assured (as readers had been assured of the historical truth of many a work of fiction) that the facts he gathered provide the basis for the story of *The Scarlet Letter*. For this reason, Hawthorne writes, his "Custom-House" preface has "a certain propriety, . . . as explaining how a large portion of the following pages came into my possession, and as offering proofs of the authenticity of [the] narrative therein contained." His own "true position," he adds, is merely that of "editor, or very little more," of *The Scarlet Letter* (p. 4).

Now everybody recognizes that this self-effacing claim of authenticity is a joke, since Hawthorne himself invented the manuscript he identifies as his source, but we need to recognize the full impact of this joke. As a mere editor, Hawthorne is claiming for his story the very sort of authority his culture approved, the authority Hawthorne turns to once once he has turned away from the conventional authority of what Jefferson called "reason and fact, plain and unadorned." But by making this claim into a joke, Hawthorne is in effect dismissing "reason and fact" every bit as much as Melville, writing to John Murray, was dismissing "acquired wisdom." The difference is that while Melville chose outright defiance, Hawthorne characteristically chooses irony, but for both writers the point is much the same. Melville rejects conventional wisdom; Hawthorne (as the title of his preface suggests) rejects accepted custom. The reader of "The Custom-House" must thus ask what sort of authority of fact, judgment, and custom.

This question seems to be answered, more or less, in the discussion of the "neutral territory." This passage occurs rather late in the preface, as part of Hawthorne's account of sitting in his parlor late at night, after a day of custom-house routine, contemplating familiar objects transformed by moonlight. This experience becomes, for him, a metaphor for the working of the imagination upon everyday reality. The objects in the room, Hawthorne writes, "are so spiritualized by the unusual light, that they seem to lose their actual substance, and become things of intellect." The moonlight invests them "with a quality of strangeness and remoteness"; defamiliarized, they come to seem as much imaginary as real. "Thus," Hawthorne concludes, "the floor of our familiar room has become a neutral territory, somewhere between the real world and fairy-land, where the Actual and the Imaginary may meet, and each imbue itself with the nature of the other" (pp. 35–6).

As I have said, this seems to be a pretty safe account of romance, apparently *reconciling* the authority of imagination with the authority of fact, of the "Actual," apparently *combining* "the real world and fairy-land." The problem, however, is that even metaphorically, this well-known passage doesn't quite make sense – at least as an account of the special art of the romancer. The imaginative quality of this scene comes from the scene itself, from the real combination of familiar objects and ethereal moonlight, and not from Hawthorne's own creative imagination; and this would seem to be the point. Hawthorne can claim to reconcile fact and fantasy because he can claim that his facts are already fantastic. If what results seems like romance, it is thus not his fault but the fault of his materials.

This idea, that romance stems not from the writer's art but from his materials, becomes even more important in Hawthorne's later prefaces. In the preface to *The Marble Faun,* for instance, he writes that "Italy, as the site of his Romance, was chiefly valuable . . . as affording a sort of poetic or fairy precinct, where actualities would not be so terribly insisted upon, as they are, and must needs be, in America" (vol. IV, p. 3). In the preface to *The Blithedale Romance,* the same argument is used to explain the use of Brook Farm as the setting for a work of fiction. "The Author," Hawthorne writes, "has ventured to make free with his old, and affectionately remembered home, at Brook Farm, as being, certainly, the most romantic episode of his own life — essentially a daydream, and yet a fact — and thus offering an available foothold between fiction and reality" (vol. III, p. 2). *The Marble Faun* and *The Blithedale Romance* are romances, this is to say, because the very facts of Italy and Brook Farm are already essentially romantic.

This is an appealing argument, allowing Hawthorne to advertise his works as romances without quite having to admit that he is himself a romancer. He thereby frees himself from personal responsibility for the romantic or imaginative quality of his works. Yet we should see this argument for what it is (and is not). It is clearly not a straightforward declaration of artistic intention, and it is certainly not a theoretical definition of a distinctively American mode of fiction. Rather, it functions as a rather devious strategy for concealing or evading the more subversive implications of being a romancer, the implications Melville, to his peril, proclaimed openly. The trouble with the descriptions of Italy, Brook Farm, and the moonlit parlor as definitions of romance is that they really don't *define* romance. Like the passage in the *Seven Gables* preface, they tell us nothing about what the romancer actually does, or about why he might wish to do it. In fact, they divert our attention from these matters, and arguably do so quite deliberately. We might recall *Webster's* definition of "red herring": "a diversion intended to distract attention from the real issue." This is precisely the function of the "neutral territory" passage in "The Custom-House"; it distracts our attention from the real issue. And the frequency with which this passage is quoted by modern critics as a definition of "romance" suggests that is has fulfilled its function admirably, allowing Hawthorne to engage in something like subversion without appearing to do anything of the sort.

Still, despite his fondness for deception and concealment, Hawthorne knew very well what the real issue was, and there are other passages in "The Custom-House," passages not very often discussed by modern critics, that hint at his true sense of the nature of romance, his true sense of the source of his own power as a fiction writer. For instance, at the close of his description of the

41

moonlit parlor, we are told: "Then, at such an hour, and with this scene before him, if a man . . . cannot dream strange things, and make them look like truth, he need never try to write romances" (p. 36). "Dream strange things, and make them look like truth": Here, for just a moment, the cat is allowed to peek out of the bag. The phrase reveals that the real source of romance is not some romantic quality in the setting but the "strange dreams" of the romancer. Even more important, the idea of reconciliation – of a "neutral territory" or an "available foothold between fiction and reality" – is revealed to be itself a fiction, a sham, a form of deception. The romancer tricks the reader into accepting his "strange dreams" by making them *look* like the sort of truth to which the reader is accustomed.

Here, for a change, we begin to get some sense of what the romancer actually does, and in this context the most interesting and revealing passages in "The Custom-House" are those describing the supposed sources for the story of *The Scarlet Letter:* the manuscript left by Surveyor Pue and the frayed letter once worn by Hester Prynne. Hawthorne begins his account of the manuscript with another joke about its supposed authority. "It should be borne carefully in mind," he reminds us, "that the main facts [of *The Scarlet Letter*] are authorized and authenticated by the document of Mr. Surveyor Pue." We are even assured that "the original papers, together with the scarlet letter itself . . . , are still in my possession, and shall be freely exhibited to whomsoever, induced by the great interest of the narrative, may desire a sight of them" (pp. 32–3). Needless to say, scholars have not yet turned up these invaluable items.

These facetious remarks are followed, however, by comments of a quite different nature. Jefferson, we recall, insisted on "reason and fact, *plain* and *unadorned*." "I must not be understood as affirming," Hawthorne writes, "that, in the dressing up of the tale, and imagining the motives and modes of passion that influenced the characters who figure in it, I have invariably confined myself within the limits of the old Surveyor's half a dozen sheets of foolscap. On the contrary, I have allowed myself, as to such points, nearly or altogether as much license as if the facts had been entirely of my own invention " (p. 33). This curiously casual progression — from "nearly" to "altogether" (presented as if they were interchangeable synonyms) to *"entirely* of my own invention" — nicely deflates the pretense of factual authenticity. It reminds us that Hawthorne is having fun with us, that his comments are often comic performances. The function of these performances, one suspects, is to mask the more subversive, even compulsive implications of a decision "to out with the Romance," but what matters first of all is simply that we recognize the irony and comedy, recognize the fact that Hawthorne, in his critical remarks, *is* performing.

In any case, whatever Hawthorne's motive may have been, there is also a serious literary significance lurking in this particular performance. In the *Seven Gables* preface, written a year after "The Custom-House," romance is distinguished by "latitude." Here the term is "license": "I have allowed myself . . . as much license as if the facts had been entirely of my own invention." Here, moreover, we are told what we are not told in the *Seven Gables* preface; we are told what this license is *for*. It allows the romancer to *imagine* "the motives and modes of passion that influenced the characters." And the special authority of romance is also, for once, identified; it is neither fact nor reason, but sympathetic "imagining."

The nature of this sympathetic imagination, and its distance from the realm of fact and custom, are revealed most clearly, in "The Custom-House," in the description of the letter of frayed scarlet cloth, supposedly bound up with Surveyor Pue's manuscript, once worn by Hester Prynne. "It strangely interested me," Hawthorne writes; and this "strangely" surely recalls his remark about the romancer's "strange dreams." "My eyes," he continues, "fastened themselves upon the old scarlet letter, and would not be turned aside. Certainly, there was some deep meaning in it, most worthy of interpretation, and which, as it were, streamed forth from the mystic symbol, subtly communicating itself to my sensibilities, but evading the analysis of my mind" (p. 31). Here the mask of objective historian or editor is dropped completely. There is even a tone of irrational obsession or compulsion in the author's confession that his eyes "fastened themselves upon the old scarlet letter, and would not be turned aside." The source of this strange fascination has nothing to do with reason or judgment, with what

43

Hawthorne here calls the "analysis of my mind," nor is there any talk here of *reconciling* fact and fantasy. Rather, this compulsive fascination derives wholly from irrational "sensibilities," from feeling and imagination. It is these "sensibilities," and not any general, rational sense of "the probable and ordinary course of man's experience," that give the author imaginative access to "the motives and modes of passion" of his characters.

The passages I have just referred to are unusual because they concern themselves with what most of Hawthorne's comments on fiction conceal or evade; they describe, or at least hint at, what the romancer actually does, and why he does it. Taken together, they indicate that the deepest significance of romance for Hawthorne had little to do with the meanings modern critics have given to the term: absence of social texture, lack of resolution, concern with Nature, and the like. These passages also suggest a notion of romance quite different from the idea of reconciliation set forth in the description of the neutral territory or in the prefaces to *The Blithedale Romance* and *The Marble Faun*. For Hawthorne, finally, the most basic authority of romance is neither "reason and fact, plain and unadorned," nor some romantic quality in certain kinds of settings, but the projected imagination of the author. Not surprisingly, this notion of the authority of romance sounds a good deal like the conventional assumptions about romance proclaimed by Herman Melville, denounced by most of Hawthorne's contemporaries, and disguised or concealed in Hawthorne's most often quoted comments on fiction.

Hawthorne described his fiction, in his preface to the 1851 edition of *Twice-Told Tales,* as an attempt "to open an intercourse with the world" (vol. IX, p. 6). His prefaces serve the same function, and this is what critics who mine them for theoretical ideas, for some theory of romance, tend to overlook. In the last analysis, these prefaces are not essays in critical definition but, as I have been arguing, dramatic, ironic, and often comic social performances, in which the author adopts a series of masks and poses in order to obscure – and yet still hint at – the true authority behind his fiction. Hawthorne knew very well what he was doing, and one guesses he enjoyed doing it. And in his preface to an 1852 story collection (*The Snow-Image and Other Tales*), he for once quite openly discusses those "superficial skimmers of pages" who insist on taking his prefaces literally. His remarks here reveal a certain detached contempt. They also, in passing, provide what may be his most complete and suggestive remarks about the art of the romancer.

Some readers, Hawthorne writes, have seen his penchant for autobiography, in his prefaces, as a sign of egotism. "A person," he replies,

> who has been burrowing . . . into the depth of our common nature, for the purposes of psychological romance, – and who pursues his researches in that dusky region, as he needs must, as well by the tact of sympathy as by the light of observation, – will smile at incurring such an imputation [i.e., of egotism] in virtue of a little preliminary talk about his external habits, his abode, his casual associates, and other matters entirely upon the surface. These things hide the man, instead of displaying him. (vol. XI, p. 4)

Having dismissed the superficiality of his literalist readers, and having described "the purposes of psychological romance" with unusual directness, Hawthorne proceeds to explain how he should properly be read. "You must make quite another kind of inquest," he writes, "and look through the whole range of [the author's] fictitious characters, good and evil, in order to detect any of his essential traits" (p. 4).

The reader, this is to say, must, like the romancer, rely on imagination, on "the tact of sympathy." If we wish to understand the author, we must understand how he has both hidden and revealed his own "essential traits" by projecting them into his characters – including, of course, the character "Nathaniel Hawthorne" who addresses us in the prefaces. The romancer dreams "strange things" and makes them "look like truth"; he manages to present unconscious fantasy in the *disguise* of socially respectable reality. This is precisely what Hawthorne does in his prefaces. It is also the "essential trait" that ties the author of "The Custom-House" most closely to his "fictitious characters" in *The Scarlet Letter*.

3

Toward the end of "The Custom-House," Hawthorne contrasts what he sees as the insubstantiality of his romance of Hester

Prynne to the superior reality of the novel he might have written about his actual experience in present-day Salem. "I might readily," he insists, "have found a more serious task."

> It was a folly, with the materiality of this daily life pressing so intrusively upon me, to attempt to fling myself back into another age; or to insist on creating the semblance of a world out of airy matter, when, at every moment, the impalpable beauty of my soap-bubble was broken by the contact of some actual circumstance. . . . A better book than I shall ever write was there; leaf after leaf presenting itself to me, just as it was written out by the reality of the flitting hour, and vanishing just as fast as written, only because my brain wanted the insight and my hand the cunning to transcribe it. (p. 37).

To the reader of *The Scarlet Letter*, this declaration seems at least odd, perhaps even disingenuous. Phrases like "airy matter," "impalpable," and "soap-bubble" hardly seem appropriate to the book they are meant to describe. The story of Hester Prynne scarcely exemplifies the fanciful insubstantiality for which "The Custom-House" takes pains to apologize in advance; on the contrary, it has all the air of "actual circumstance."

To be sure, there are flights of allegorical fancifulness in the book, notably in connection with little Pearl, and all the talk of the mystic "elf-child" and her natural affinity for sunshine is inevitably unpalatable to modern readers trained on realistic fiction. Still, *The Scarlet Letter* is, in the most fundamental respects, a significantly realistic work of fiction.[16] Its greatest importance to the history of fiction in English is probably its development of analytical, psychological realism, especially in its probing and elaboration of the conscious and unconscious motives and feelings of Hester Prynne and Arthur Dimmesdale. In this respect, it foreshadows (as it also influenced) the work of such later psychological realists as George Eliot and Henry James. Moreover, in its treatment of Puritan history, as Michael Colacurcio and others have persuasively demonstrated, *The Scarlet Letter* is thoroughly and realistically concerned with both the details and the meaning of the New England past.[17] The account of romance in "The Custom-House" seems, then, curiously inappropriate to the book it claims to describe.

From another point of view, however, the discussion of romance in "The Custom-House" is a particularly appropriate gateway to the world of *The Scarlet Letter*. For while *The Scarlet Letter*, as a work of prose fiction, may seem to have little in common with the sort of romance Hawthorne describes in his preface, the behavior of the characters in the book, especially that of Arthur Dimmesdale and Hester Prynne, has a great deal in common with the duplicitous deception that, as Hawthorne describes and impersonates him in "The Custom-House," characterizes the behavior of the romancer. To read *The Scarlet Letter* as some sort of *kunstlerroman*, as an allegorical exploration of the nature and sources of "psychological romance," is to risk distorting its solidly real concern with general human psychology and Puritan history. Yet, both Dimmesdale and Hester do function in the book, in effect, as artists, manipulating appearances – much like the Hawthorne of the prefaces – in order to mediate between their own subversive impulses and the orthodox expectations of the society in which they live their public lives.[18]

From the very beginning, Dimmesdale sets out to deceive – egregiously deceive – those superficial proponents of Puritan orthodoxy whose need to see him as pious is comparable to the need of Hawthorne's readers to see him, in Melville's phrase, as "a man who means no meanings." When we first see Dimmesdale, he is openly exhorting Hester to name her child's father while, secretly, of course, urging her to do just the opposite; already, at the outset, he is a master of doublespeak. And his celebrated sermons, like Hawthorne's prefaces, permit him to confess without taking responsibility for what he is confessing. His hearers, we are told, "little guessed what deadly purport lurked in [his] self-condemning words," and this deception is quite deliberate: "The minister well knew – subtle, but remorseful hypocrite that he was! – the light in which his vague confession would be viewed" (vol. I, p. 144). Dimmesdale would thus appear to succeed, as Melville thought Hawthorne succeeded, in indulging "instinct" without seeming, at least publicly, to reject "acquired wisdom."

The problem, of course, is that the person Dimmesdale succeeds in deceiving above all is himself. If he is a kind of artist, he is nonetheless unable to regard either the inward motive or the outward expression of his art as anything but falsehood; unlike the subversive romancer, he fully shares his society's equation of the source of his art — passionate, forbidden "impulse" — with sin. "As concerns the good which I may appear to do," he insists to Hester when they finally meet in the forest, "I have no faith in it. It must needs be a delusion. . . . I have laughed, in bitterness and agony of heart, at the contrast between what I seem and what I am" (p. 191).

Dimmesdale may dream strange things and make them look like truth, but he himself cannot *believe* in their truth. He does not indulge his forbidden fantasies; he simply represses them. And even as he distinguishes between "what I seem and what I am," he becomes hopelessly confused. "No man," we are told, "for any considerable period, can wear one face to himself, and another to the multitude, without finally getting bewildered as to which may be the true" (p. 216). Returning from the forest, Dimmesdale imagines that he has finally determined to release "the inner man," to act on his "impulses," to fling his old self down (as Hester has just thrown off her letter and her cap) "like a cast-off garment," but his understanding of this "revolution in the sphere of thought and feeling" reveals only ever-deepening perplexity. "At every step," we are told, "he was incited to do some strange, wild, wicked thing or other, with a sense that it would be at once involuntary and intentional; in spite of himself, yet growing out of a profounder self than that which opposed the impulse" (p. 217).

Dimmesdale might appear, in the climax of the story, to have resolved the conflict between the competing truths of inner impulse and outward expression. Following his election sermon — beneath whose rhetoric of social progress Hester hears a "low undertone" of "the complaint of a human heart, sorrow-laden, perchance guilty, telling its secret" (p. 243) — he does join Hester and Pearl on the scaffold, to confess his sin openly at last. He does literally cast off the garment of deception, removing the ministerial band to reveal his own scarlet letter. Yet we should remember that the art of the romancer, for the Hawthorne of the prefaces, involves not the casting off of masks — he vows at the beginning of "The Custom-House," for instance, to "keep the inmost Me behind its veil" (p. 4) — but the manipulation of appearances to *insinuate* deeper "truths." We should also recognize that Dimmesdale's resolution of his confusion at the close is only apparent. The election sermon itself is produced out of the same perplexity Dimmesdale brought back from the forest, "at once involuntary and intentional." If it gives expression to "an impulsive flow of thought and emotion," it nevertheless does so through the medium of an officially sanctioned form – a form, moreover, that Dimmesdale, who "fancied himself inspired," must still believe to be officially sanctioned. It is not that Dimmesdale (like the arch romancer of the prefaces) subverts orthodoxy by pretending to adhere to it; rather, he himself can acknowledge "impulse" and "emotion" only when they are disguised as divine "inspiration" – wondering all the while "that Heaven should see fit to transmit the grand and solemn music of its oracles through so foul an organ-pipe as he" (p. 225). Here Hawthorne's irony is devastating. Dimmesdale cannot recognize the significant sexual pun in "organ-pipe." Even in the privacy of his own thoughts, he must continue to distinguish between his "sin" and the source of his "artistic" power.

Dimmesdale's final confession, for all of its apparent sincerity, is also fraught with irony. He casts off imposture, after all, in an elaborately staged *performance;* he turns privacy into public spectacle. What he reveals, we should also recognize, is less an inner "impulse" than an outward *sign,* a letter – the same letter that Hester has been wearing, all along, *as* a garment. Moreover, as we learn in the "Conclusion," Dimmesdale's confession is sufficiently equivocal so as to allow "certain persons, who were spectators of the whole scene" (p. 259), to interpret it just as his earlier "confessions" were interpreted: as a general dramatization of sinfulness rather than as a personal confession of a specific sin. From beginning to end, then, it would seem that Dimmesdale's deception remains self-deception. Hawthorne, in his preface to *The Snow-Image and Other Tales,* distinguishes between "external habits" and "essential traits." Dimmesdale is never able to determine which is which. We might thus understand him as a kind of false or failed romancer, ultimately less an artist than a text, a text that he himself can neither control nor even read.

If any character in *The Scarlet Letter* learns to control the interplay of "external" and "essential," to become the sort of romancer Hawthorne hints at in his prefaces, that character is Hester Prynne. She does not, however, learn this lesson all at once. At the outset, she is as confused as Dimmesdale, albeit in a somewhat different fashion, about the relationship between what she seems and what she is. Hester climbs the scaffold, at the beginning of the story, as a central figure in an allegorical social drama – what contemporary sociologists would call a symbolic degradation ritual – and she thinks of her performance in overtly theatrical terms. "Knowing well her part," we are told, "she ascended a flight of wooden steps, and was thus displayed to the surrounding multitude" (p. 55–6). All other conceptions of her identity are engulfed by her allegorical, deviant social role, and she herself fully conspires, or attempts to conspire, in this eradication of her inner personality: "She turned her eyes downward at the scarlet letter, and even touched it with her finger, to assure herself that the infant and the shame were real. Yes! – these were her realities, – all else had vanished!" (p. 59). "In this manner," the narrator later writes, once again enforcing the metaphor of theatrical artifice, "Hester Prynne came to have a part to perform in the world" (p. 84).

Hester, according to the narrator, gives up her "individuality" in order to become "the general symbol at which the preacher and moralist might point, and in which they might vivify and embody their images of woman's frailty and sinful passion" (p. 79). Hester is defined as their text, and she attempts to read herself at their valuation. Yet Hester's extirpation of her "individuality," of her inner life of "impulse," is hardly so complete or successful as she wishes to believe. It is to this repressed "impulse," for instance, that she gives covert expression through the art of needlework, with which she adorns her scarlet letter and her daughter, Pearl. (We should also here recall Hawthorne's comments in "The Custom-House" about "the dressing up of the tale, and imagining the motives and modes of passion that influenced the characters who figure in it.") For all of Hester's outward social conformity, we are told, her needlework "appeared to have also a deeper meaning"; "it might have been a mode of expressing, and therefore soothing, the passion of her life" (p. 83–4). Here Hester seems very much a figure of the romancer, simultaneously expressing and concealing the content of her strange dreams.

Like Dimmesdale, however, Hester is at this point mainly concerned with concealing her dreams from herself. To the extent that her needlework expresses "the passion of her life," we are told, "she rejected it as sin" (p. 84). Nor can she face openly, even in the privacy of her own thoughts, the idea that one of her motives for staying in Boston may be her enduring love for Arthur Dimmesdale:

> She barely looked the idea in the face, and hastened to bar it in its dungeon. What she compelled herself to believe, – what, finally, she reasoned upon, as her motive for continuing a resident of New England, – was half a truth, and half a self-delusion. Here, she said to herself, had been the scene of her guilt, and here should be the scene of her earthly punishment; and so, perchance, the torture of her daily shame would at length purge her soul, and work out another purity than that which she had lost; more saint-like, because the result of martyrdom. (p. 80)

This surely sounds like the Dimmesdale who can stand no discrepancy between "what I seem" and "what I am."

Nevertheless, by the time Pearl has reached the age of seven, Hester has changed, and seems much more like the deliberately duplicitous romancer of Hawthorne's prefaces. The great summary chapter of psychological and social analysis, "Another View of Hester," describes a woman who wears one face to herself and another to society, but who remains very much aware (unlike Dimmesdale) of the different ways in which each of these faces is true. "She never battled with the public," we are told, "but submitted uncomplainingly to its worst usage" (p. 160). She has even convinced the public that her embroidered letter – through which she has long expressed and soothed "the passion of her life" – is "the token, not of that one sin, for which she had borne so long and dreary a penance, but of her many good deeds since" (p. 162).

Yet, behind this mask of "acquired wisdom," Hester has been nurturing her "instinct," nurturing a thoroughly subversive sense of her "individuality." "The world's law," we are told, "was no law for her mind. . . . Hester Prynne . . . assumed a freedom of

51

speculation . . . which our forefathers, had they known of it, would have held to be a deadlier crime than that stigmatized by the scarlet letter." But they do not know of it; they are as deceived – as egregiously deceived – as were, so Melville thought, Hawthorne's "superficial" readers. "It is remarkable," writes the narrator, "that persons who speculate the most boldly often conform with the most perfect quietude to the external regulations of society" (p. 164). Hester dreams strange things and makes them look like truth; and what matters most, she clearly (unlike Dimmesdale) understands what she is doing.

She still, however, has another lesson to learn. In the forest, she determines to cast off the arts of deception, to act openly on the truths of "impulse" and "individuality." "See!" she proclaims, throwing off the scarlet letter, "With this symbol, I undo it all, and make it as it had never been!" (p. 202). In this moment, she drops the duplicitous mode of Hawthorne for the open defiance of Melville. In the event, of course, this open rebellion is frustrated: Hester must reassume the scarlet letter – first to placate Pearl, then to conceal from the town her plan to escape with Dimmesdale – and Dimmesdale's confession and death undermine this plan permanently. But there is a deeper meaning in the frustration of Hester's open rebellion, her avowal of overt sincerity. Hester, in the forest, is doing what Dimmesdale does in his final confession on the scaffold: She is turning inner feeling, defined all along by its repression and concealment, into outward display, public spectacle. She thereby betrays the most essential character of this feeling, of her experience of this feeling. Her repudiation of symbolism in the name of freedom – "See! With this symbol, I undo it all!" – is itself, inevitably, a symbolic gesture. Pearl, who has all along been tied to her mother as a symbol simultaneously of inward rebellion and outward conformity, is right to refuse to recognize this new Hester.

When Hester returns to Boston in the book's "Conclusion," she has returned as well to something like the art of deception described in "Another View of Hester." She finds "a more real life," we are told, "here, in New England, than in that unknown region where Pearl had found a home. Here had been her sin; here, her sorrow; and here was yet to be her penitence" (pp. 262–3). This sounds ominously like the self-deceiving Hester, earlier, to whom only the tokens of shame were "realities," the Hester who masked her abiding passion, even from herself, in the language of "guilt," "earthly punishment," and "martyrdom"; but there are major differences. For one thing, this language now seems to apply truly to Hester's feelings; she is now apparently sincerely penitent, or at least bereft of any opportunity to gratify her love for Dimmesdale. What may be even more important is that she has now "resumed, – of her own free will, for not the sternest magistrate of that iron period would have imposed it, – resumed the symbol of which we have related so dark a tale" (p. 263). The crucial term here is "free will": Paradoxically enough, it is by *forsaking* open rebellion, by reassuming her part in society, that Hester is at last able to realize her individuality and freedom. And this paradox lies at the heart, not only of Hester's story, but of Hawthorne's conception of the art of fiction.

Nor does outward conformity prevent Hester from proclaiming her quite revolutionary and "firm belief, that, at some brighter period, when the world should have grown ripe for it, in Heaven's own time, a new truth would be revealed, in order to establish the whole relation between man and woman on a surer ground of mutual happiness" (p. 263). To be sure, Hester, in view of her own sinfulness, renounces all pretension to being herself the "destined prophetess" of this new order, but we should attend to the irony here. It is her outwardly humble renunciation of this role that allows her, in fact, to play it; for in what sense is a woman who announces a "firm belief" in a new order *not* a "prophetess"?

Seeking a moral for his story, Hawthorne's narrator proclaims, in the "Conclusion": "Be true! Be true! Be true! Show freely to the world, if not your worst, yet some trait whereby the worst may be inferred!" (p. 260). What matters most about this avowal of sincerity is the speed with which it is qualified, the speed with which a call for sincere openness succumbs to a recognition of the need for indirection; and in this qualification we see both the truth of Hester's story and the central assumption underlying Hawthorne's writing about romance. Melville's open avowal of instinct, as he himself rapidly discovered, led not only to alienation but to distortion. Hawthorne, like Hester, rebels rather through indirection, through ironic subversion, through showing not the worst but something whereby the worst might be inferred – or not inferred, for that matter, at least by the "superficial skimmer of pages." We can only speculate about *why* Hawthorne was impelled toward subversion, but what matters is that we recognize the subversive impulse, and the ways this impulse is managed and masked, in both his fiction and his critical writing. For as Melville was one of the first to recognize, the art of the romancer, for Hawthorne, was above all an art of deception.

NOTES

1 "Hawthorne and His *Mosses*," in Jay Leyda, ed., *The Portable Melville* (New York: Viking, 1952), pp. 404–6, 418.

2 The fountainhead of this view of Hawthorne in twentieth-century criticism is D. H. Lawrence's *Studies in Classic American Literature* (Garden City, N.Y.: Doubleday, 1923). "You *must* look through the surface of American art," Lawrence writes in his discussion of *The Scarlet Letter*, "and see the inner diabolism of the symbolic meaning." "That blue-eyed darling Nathaniel," he continues, "knew disagreeable things in his inner soul. He was careful to send them out in disguise" (p. 93).

3 *Webster's Third New International Dictionary of the English Language Unabridged* (Springfield, Ill.: G.&C. Merriam, 1967), p. 1902.

4 All parenthetical volume and page references are to *The Centenary Edition of the Works of Nathaniel Hawthorne* (Columbus: Ohio State University Press, 1962ff.).

5 See, for instance, Henry James, *Hawthorne* (1879), reprinted in Edmund Wilson, ed., *The Shock of Recognition* (New York: Random House, 1943), pp. 427–565; and William Dean Howells, *Literary Friends and Acquaintance*, ed. David F. Hiatt and Edwin H. Cady (Bloomington: Indiana University Press), esp. pp. 47–53. See, too, Richard H. Brodhead, "Hawthorne Among the Realists: The Case of Howells," in Eric J. Sundquist, ed., *American Realism: New Essays* (Baltimore: Johns Hopkins University Press, 1982), pp. 25–41.

6 Lionel Trilling, "Manners, Morals, and the Novel," reprinted in *The Liberal Imagination* (New York: Scribner's, 1950), p. 212.

7 Richard Chase, *The American Novel and Its Tradition* (Garden City, N.Y.: Doubleday, 1957), p. xii; F. R. Leavis, *The Great Tradition* (London: Chatto & Windus, 1948); Perry Miller, "The Romance and the

Novel," in *Nature's Nation* (Cambridge, Mass.: Harvard University Press, 1967), pp. 241–78; Northrop Frye, *Anatomy of Criticism* (Princeton, N.J.: Princeton University Press, 1957); Joel Porte, *The Romance in America* (Middletown, Conn.: Wesleyan University Press, 1969), p. ix. My own book on this subject, *The Development of American Romance: The Sacrifice of Relation* (Chicago: University of Chicago Press, 1980), is concerned less with the existence (or nonexistence) of a romance tradition in pre–Civil War America than with the question of what pre–Civil War Americans meant when they used the term "romance," and with how the meanings clustered around the term influenced the thought and fiction of so-called American romancers.

8 For objections to the romance hypothesis see, for instance, Richard Poirier, *A World Elsewhere: The Place of Style in American Literature* (New York: Oxford University Press, 1966), pp. 8–11; David H. Hirsch, *Reality and Idea in the Early American Novel* (The Hague: Mouton, 1971), pp. 32–48; Nicolaus Mills, *American and English Fiction in the Nineteenth Century: An Antigenre Critique and Comparison* (Bloomington: Indiana University Press, 1973); and Robert Merrill, "Another Look at the American Romance," *Modern Philology* 78 (May, 1981): 379–92.

9 Chase, *The American Novel and Its Tradition,* p. 18. On Chase's reversal of Hawthorne's meaning in the preface to *The Marble Faun,* see Mills, *American and English Fiction in the Nineteenth Century,* p. 25.

10 Trilling, *The Liberal Imagination,* p. 212; Chase, *The American Novel and Its Tradition,* p. 2; Miller, *Nature's Nation,* p. 247.

11 In "The Romance and the Novel," Perry Miller seems to find Melville's definition of "romance" (especially in a famous 1848 letter to John Murray, to which I refer below) more central than Hawthorne's various definitions. Still, he does quote the *Seven Gables* preface, and appears to find it in accord with what he takes Melville to be saying (*Nature's Nation,* p. 245.)

12 Nina Baym, *Novels, Readers, and Reviewers: Responses to Fiction in Antebellum America* (Ithaca, N.Y.: Cornell University Press, 1984), pp. 225–35.

13 Thomas Jefferson to Nathaniel Burwell, March 14, 1818, in Paul Leicester Ford, ed., *The Works of Thomas Jefferson,* vol. 10 (New York: Putnam, 1899), pp. 104–5. On hostility toward fiction and imagination in eighteenth and early nineteenth-century America, see William Charvat, *The Origins of American Critical Thought, 1810–1835* (Philadelphia: University of Pennsylvania Press, 1936); my own *The Development of American Romance: The Sacrifice of Relation,* particularly pp. 9–14; and especially Terence Martin, *The Instructed Vision: Scottish Com-*

mon Sense Philosophy and the Origins of American Fiction (Bloomington: University of Indiana Press, 1961).

14 The Letters of Herman Melville, ed. Merrell R. Davis and William H. Gilman (New Haven, Conn.: Yale University Press, 1960), p. 71.

15 For an excellent account of Melville's relationship to his reading public, see William Charvat, "Melville," in Matthew J. Bruccoli, ed., The Profession of Authorship in Amerca, 1800–1870 (Columbus: Ohio State University Press, 1969), pp. 204–61.

16 A belief in the fundamentally novelistic quality of The Scarlet Letter is shared, paradoxically enough, by both opponents and proponents of the romance hypothesis. Robert Merrill attacks the romance approach to The Scarlet Letter in "Another Look at the American Romance"; yet even Richard Chase, Merrill's principal target, insists that The Scarlet Letter "is primarily a novel" – with only elements of romance (The American Novel and Its Tradition, p. 68).

17 Michael J. Colacurcio, "Footsteps of Ann Hutchinson: The Context of The Scarlet Letter," ELH 39 (Sept., 1973): 459–94. For an earlier consideration of Hawthorne that also takes seriously his concern with history, see Q. D. Leavis, "Hawthorne as Poet," Sewanee Review 59 (Spring, Summer, 1951): 180–205, 426–58. For my own views on this matter see The Development of American Romance, pp. 169–79, and Hawthorne and the Historical Romance of New England (Princeton, N.J.: Princeton University Press, 1971), pp. 126–46, 173–90.

18 The notion that various characters in The Scarlet Letter function in one way or another as artists is widespread. It is particularly central to Joel Porte's reading of the book in The Romance in America, pp. 98–114.

3

Hester's Labyrinth: Transcendental Rhetoric in Puritan Boston

DAVID VAN LEER

FIRST novels are almost inevitably too full, as the author tries to pack all his ideas into a single work. Surely plenitude is the condition of *The Scarlet Letter*. Many of Hawthorne's themes and narrative techniques from the tales reappear in the book, however briefly, and the attentive reader hears echoes of (at least) "My Kinsman, Major Molineux," "Young Goodman Brown," "Fancy's Show Box," "Lady Eleanore's Mantle," "The Birth-mark," "Egotism; or, The Bosom-Serpent," and "The Christmas Banquet."[1] The tight control Hawthorne exercises over the novel's structure is less evident in its thematic elements; some ideas seem inappropriate, others irrelevant, even vestigial. Moreover, the wildly allusive narration presents these themes in such a curious mix of Puritan rhetoric and more contemporary formulations that one almost despairs of finding the story's center amid the multitude of ideas and voices.

Yet unlike most first novels, *The Scarlet Letter* is also a masterpiece, the work of a mature artist fully in control of his craft. It is probably unwise, then, to attribute this babel of voices merely to the overenthusiasm of the neophyte romancer. Throughout the tales, Hawthorne's use of a "twice-told" narration, his reformulation of other people's stories, demands that we attend to the teller as well as the tale – to ask who first interpreted the cutting of a maypole as the symbolic castration of America, or by whose lights a mechanical butterfly epitomized the confrontation between the Beautiful and Reality. Everywhere in the tales, the philosophical assumptions of Hawthorne's narrators are as important as the moral judgments they make. So, in *The Scarlet Letter*, a narration that at times seems indecisive – an intellectual cacophony – is itself part of the book's characterization of the problem. And close attention to the method of the narrative – the *how* of the book – may help simplify what at first appear to be its protean complexities – its *what*.

1

Perhaps the easiest place to discover this mixing of rhetorics is in the verbal anachronisms – the narrator's use of a contemporary word or concept that would not have been available in the seventeenth century. Some of this terminology, of course, may mark occasional carelessness on Hawthorne's part. But as with the novel's celebrated historical "mistakes," most of these words call attention to themselves in a way that would have no more escaped a midcentury reader than did James's use of slang fifty years later.[2] Many of the misused terms derive from contemporary science and pseudoscience. The characterization of celestial portents as "awful hieroglyphics" and Pearl herself as a "living hieroglyphic" registers the revived interest in Egyptology after Champollion's deciphering of the Rosetta stone in 1822 (pp. 155, 207).[3] Hester's search in Pearl's nature for some dark peculiarity that would "correspond" to her own guilt, and the narrator's notion that in Hester's heart and countenance might be seen a "corresponding development" allude to the popularity of spiritual dictionaries, most closely associated with Emanuel Swedenborg's theory of the symbolic "correspondences" between spiritual and natural facts (pp. 90, 227).[4] Similarly, the vogue of phrenology is apparent in Hester's "combative" energy (p. 78), and the new science of "physiognomy" is used to illuminate the character of the Puritan elders, Mistress Hibbins, and Pearl (pp. 49, 116, 106, 212).[5]

Even words that do not seem inappropriate in a seventeenth-century context are at times defined as such by the narration. The age is said to be one in which "what we call talent" carried far less weight than the more characteristically Puritan virtues of stability and dignity (p. 237). And Hester's embroidery becomes not simply popular but "what would now be termed the fashion" (p. 82). This penchant for anachronistic vocabulary – the habit of placing words within Jamesian quotation marks – problematizes even those words not explicitly so identified. The narrator's implication that "fashion" is a modern concept makes it all the more difficult to determine the significance of characterizing Bellingham's ruff as "in the antiquated fashion of King James's reign" (p. 108): Is it merely that the ruff is twenty years out of date? Or that all seventeenth-century ruffs look antiquated from the viewpoint of the mid-nineteenth century? Or that the very notion of fashionableness has no referent in a culture that does not even have the word in its modern sense? And since words like "alchemy" and "incredulity" have very different meanings in the seventeenth and nineteenth centuries, phrases like the "alchemy of quiet malice" or "modern incredulity" turn into sly oxymorons (pp. 85, 88). In the dual focus of his historical position, the narrator almost seems to be trying to graft a lively, seventeenth-century understanding of alchemy and credulity onto what were for the nineteenth century largely dead metaphors.[6] By the time we get to the characterization of the Puritans and Dimmesdale as "gloomy" or "morbid" or "sorrowful," it becomes virtually impossible to decide whether these words are used in a neutral seventeenth-century sense or as code terms of a more contemporary, Romantic angst.[7]

Striking though they may be, however, these verbal anachronisms are finally only a specific form of a more subtle intellectual anachronism – one in which words available to the seventeenth century define ideological positions that are unlikely, even impossible. In describing the class of minister to which Dimmesdale "most probably" belongs, the narrator says of those who are pure, even ethereal, yet without inspiration: "All that they lacked was the gift that descended upon the chosen disciples, at Pentecost, in tongues of flame; symbolizing, it would seem, not the power of speech in foreign and unknown languages, but that of addressing the whole human brotherhood in the heart's native language" (pp. 141–2). The category is one a Puritan would have understood – that of the purely "civil" man unregenerated by God's grace. And the typological reading of Pentecost as the gift of ministerial grace seems orthodox enough. But the tone is wrong. What the narrator feels to be a minor weakness would be decried by most Puritans as the ruinous influence of an unconverted ministry. And whatever the tone, no Puritan would ever be so confident of salvation as to conflate the gift of grace with the discovery of the "heart's native language."[8]

A similar mix of Calvinist and Romantic categories characterizes Hester's relation to Pearl. Throughout the book, Hester searches in Pearl for the physical signs of her own spiritual weakness.

> Hester could only account for the child's character – and even then, most vaguely and imperfectly – by recalling what she herself had been, during that momentous period while Pearl was imbibing her soul from the spiritual world, and her bodily frame from its material of earth. The mother's impassioned state had been the medium through which were transmitted to the unborn infant the rays of its moral life. (p. 91)

This theory of the literal continuity between spirit and matter is, of course, present in the seventeenth century, although it reaches its peak somewhat after the decade of the 1640s, in which the story is set. The notion that a pregnant woman's mental state might physically affect the fetus led to the preoccupation with birthmarks and monstrous births in such orthodox Puritans as John Winthrop, Jr., and Cotton Mather (and, of course, finds its fictional expression in Hawthorne's own tale, "The Birth-mark").[9] Yet Hester's description of the mechanics of the process would not be congenial to any form of Calvinism. It is unlikely that a Puritan would view creation as a compounding of material body and spiritual soul; even less so that the child itself would have so active a role in the "imbibing." And it would be quite simply heretical to imagine that the mother, whether or not the "medium" of moral transmission, might in her own passion alter the moral dimension that is God's alone to give.[10]

The apparent modernization of traditional Puritan concepts is most evident, however, in neither Dimmesdale's relation to the Pentecost nor Hester's to birthmarks, but in the narrator's account of the Providential theory of history:

> It was, indeed, a majestic idea, that the destiny of nations should be revealed, in these awful hieroglyphics, on the cope of heaven. A scroll so wide might not be deemed too expansive for Providence to write a people's doom upon . . . But what shall we say, when an individual discovers a revelation, addressed to himself alone, on the same vast sheet of record! In such a case, it could only be the symptom of a highly disordered mental state, when a man, ren-

dered morbidly self-contemplative by long, intense, and secret pain, had extended his egotism over the whole expanse of nature, until the firmament itself should appear no more than a fitting page for his soul's history and fate. (p. 155)

As with the earlier passages, the narrator's explanation of the theory is traditional enough. The context within which he presents it, however, is more surprising. The narrator accepts as a "majestic idea" that the destiny of a nation could be "revealed" in the "awful hieroglyphics" of heaven. It is only when the "revelation" is purely personal – addressed to "the faith of some lonely eyewitness, who beheld the wonder through the colored, magnifying, and distorting medium of his imagination" – that the account seems suspect. In these circumstances, a self-aggrandizing theory of history turns into "the symptom of a highly disordered mental state," whose cause is not a problematic notion of God's special covenant with America, but a "long, intense, and secret pain" that renders the individual "morbidly self-contemplative." In part, of course, the narrator's equation of Providential history with egotism implicitly challenges the notion of a national destiny as much as it does a sense of private revelation. Yet the reductiveness of his conclusion – that the historical misinterpretation is like (or even caused by) bodily malfunctioning – seems to mark his own intellectual limitations as much as those of Puritan historiography.

The narrator's explanation is perhaps even more suggestive. For here, and throughout the novel, the narrator does not merely modernize traditional Puritan concepts. Even as he translates them out of an overdetermined theological context, he translates them into another no less determined epistemological one. In speaking of the credibility of the lonely eyewitness, for example, he does not merely universalize Puritan theory, but conflates history and perception in a way characteristic of Romantic thought from Wordsworth on, and unique to it. The very reference to the imagination as a "colored, magnifying, and distorting medium" aligns his theory, perhaps explicitly, with Emerson's famous definition of subjectivity in "Experience" as the negative discovery of "these colored and distorting lenses which we are."[11]

So, in fact, all of the narrator's modernizations seem to share a certain family resemblance, generally Romantic and perhaps even specifically Transcendental. Hester's flinging away the scarlet letter "into infinite space" in the forest scene may recall the early moment in Emerson's *Nature* when, returning to faith and reason "in the woods," man is uplifted "into infinite space."[12] Similarly, the language of transparency and especially of "vanishing," so ubiquitous in the novel, may owe something to Emerson's notorious claim to be able to make disagreeable appearances "vanish."[13] Most explicitly, Hester's "wander[ing] without a clew in the dark labyrinth of mind" seems to echo Emerson's fear that, without a divine influx, idealism "leaves me in the splendid labyrinth of my perceptions, to wander without end" (p. 166; cf. CW, vol. I, p. 37).

The last echo of Emerson's wandering in the splendid labyrinth with Hester's wandering in the dark one seems unmistakable, and introduces into the novel a string of Romantic metaphors about wanderings and labyrinths.[14] Yet this un−Calvinist interpretation of Hester's confusion as epistemological, even perceptual, is immediately coupled with her more Puritan decision to resolve her anxiety about justification perversely by murdering Pearl and thereby resting assured in her damnation.[15] Clearly, Hester is not simply a proto-Romantic caught in a Puritan society: As no Calvinist would worry about the labyrinth of the mind, so no Transcendentalist would see murder as a salvation from uncertainty.[16] But just as clearly, the interpenetration of the two vocabularies – moral and epistemological, Puritan and Transcendental – is disorienting, and forces us to ask what exactly is the intellectual context of Hester's dilemma.

2

The point is not to see *The Scarlet Letter* as a tale of Puritan New England "twice-told" by Emerson. Nor, more generally, is it to claim that the book offers a version of the modern preoccupation with the Puritan origins of American Romanticism – Hawthorne's account of the intellectual journey from Edwards to Emerson. Yet it is important to recognize that a work that is in some senses scrupulously faithful to the intellectual categories of Calvinism is in others explicitly and even arrogantly contemptuous of that very kind of historical precision. Moreover, the inconsistency does not

seem a function of characterization: Dimmesdale, Hester, Chillingworth, and Pearl all evince both Puritan and Transcendental traits.
Instead, the conflation seems more general throughout the narration, involving less the individual psychologies of the characters
than the character of the narration itself. To determine the nature
of that narration, and of the translations the narrator makes in
retelling his Puritan tale, we must turn to the one section where
the narrator ostensibly speaks in his own voice – the introductory
essay "The Custom-House."[17]

With the memory of the subtle Emersonianism of the novel
proper ringing in our ears, it is hard to miss that this introductory
essay too betrays an unexpected Transcendental bias. The Emersonian vocabulary of "vanishings" and "transparency" appears regularly in the essay, usually in an ironic context. Emerson's famous
doctrine of "self-reliance" is said to open up equally Emersonian
"prospects," and the denial of books derives from a similar dismissal in "The American Scholar" (pp. 25–6, 39). Perhaps the
somber aspect of the novel "ungladdened" by genial sunshine –
and especially the unusual participle – owe something to Emerson's famous sensation in the forest of being "glad to the brink of
fear" (p. 43).[18] And surely his initial definition of his "perfectly
sympathetic" audience as a "divided segment" – the counterpart
of the "writer's own nature," the contact with which will "complete his circle of existence" (pp. 3–4) – looks back not only to
Aristophanes's comic account of love in *The Symposium* but to a
more proximate (and more serious) source in Emerson's myth of
the One Man.[19]

But the truly Transcendental moment is that which ends the
introductory section – and denies it. Having presented his reasons
for autobiography, the narrator immediately turns around to insist
even here on his anonymity: "we may prate of the circumstances
that lie around us, and even of ourself, but still keep the inmost Me
behind its veil" (p. 4). The point is, of course, familiar from
Hawthorne's other statements about his habitual reticence. The
tone, however, is unclear. Usually Hawthorne defends his privacy
in terms of decorum. At the end of "The Old Manse," for example,
the narrator implies that self-revelation is simply too graphic. "So
far as I am a man of really individual attributes, I veil my face; nor

am I, nor have I ever been, one of those supremely hospitable people, who serve up their own hearts, delicately fried, with brain-sauce, as a tidbit for their beloved public" (vol. X, p. 33).[20] To insist here, then, that true autobiography is essentially a variety of unpardonable sin or violation of the sanctum sanctorum seems at best melodramatic and at worst deeply confused on the meaning of personality. As before, the difference in tone – between speaking of fried organs and an inmost Me – seems attributable to the Emersonian diction, and especially his dichotomy between ME and NOT ME from which it pretty clearly derives.[21]

The frequency of these Emersonian echoes is puzzling, especially from a narrator who explicitly claims to have rejected Emerson, Alcott, and the other Transcendentalists. Although inconclusive in themselves, however, the echoes should at least warn against equating this narrator too quickly with Hawthorne – and alert us to the other tonal peculiarities in this introductory narrative. Some of the narrator's feebler attempts at wit seem to backfire, and tell more against him than against their intended object. His admission concerning the Inspector – that he could not conceive "how he should exist hereafter, so earthy and sensuous did he seem" (p. 18) – suggests a foolishly literal reading of Christian principles of moderation: the claim that it is easier for a camel to go through the eye of a needle than for a fat man to enter into the kingdom of God. Moreover, given the novel's sophisticated attitude toward feminism and especially woman's work, it is difficult to take seriously the narrator's reference to "womankind, with her tools of magic, the broom and mop" (p. 7).[22] Most strikingly, it is hard to know what to do with the narrator's claim to follow faithfully the example of Pope's *Memoirs of P. P.* The whole point of that mock autobiography is to expose the boorishness of the scatologically named biographer; and following his example is an admission of one's own incompetence as witness.

More important than these oddly self-incriminating solecisms is the narrator's confusion about what he does in the introduction and what happens in the novel. Bemoaning the death of his imagination in the Custom-House, the narrator complains:

> It was a folly, with the materiality of this daily life pressing so
> intrusively upon me, to attempt to fling myself back into another

age; or to insist on creating the semblance of a world out of airy matter, when, at every moment, the impalpable beauty of my soap-bubble was broken by the rude contact of actual circumstance. (p. 37)

The vaguely Transcendental melodrama of the language, and especially the oxymoron "airy matter," might itself make us suspect his formulation. But more simply, one wonders if he has really failed at all. The passage concludes:

> The page of life that was spread out before me seemed dull and commonplace, only because I had not fathomed its deeper import. A better book than I shall ever write was there; leaf after leaf presenting itself to me, just as it was written out by the reality of the flitting hour, and vanishing as fast as written, only because my brain wanted the insight and my hand the cunning to transcribe it. (p. 37)

Yet, in fact, his claim to be unable to write such a book – for which "these perceptions have come too late" – is literally untrue. "The Custom-House" itself, although not a book, is surely the successful product of that very search for "the true and indestructible value that lay hidden in the petty and wearisome incidents, and ordinary characters, with which I was now conversant" (p. 37). Similarly, the whole definition of the historian's project as the creation of a past out of airy matter is ironically undercut by the recognition that the preface contains within it an historical fiction both successful and unproblematically material – the re-creation of the Old General's triumph at Ticonderoga.

A more subtle contradiction informs the narrator's approach to the seventeenth century. When the narrator confronts his Puritan ancestors, they speak to his Romantic guilt about the triviality of his calling. "'A writer of story-books! What kind of a business in life, – what mode of glorifying God, or being serviceable to mankind in his day and generation, – may that be?'" (p. 10). Yet these ghostly ancestors (not historical figures but projections of the narrator's own vocational crisis) in fact have a very different relation to literature than do the Puritans in the novel. They object that writers are "idle," insufficiently concerned with glorifying God and serving man. The novel's Puritans are not so puritanical. They repeatedly enjoy the material comforts that the preface's Puritans disdain.[23] Moreover, they are, if anything, too aware of the value of literature. Hester's letter is, for them, not idle but intensely meaningful; and the shame of her embroidery is not that she has wasted time on the trivial but that she has tampered with a divinely given significance. For these Puritans, as for the Bay Psalm editors, writing is not idleness but hubris: God's altar needs not our polishings, but only because it is already consecrated.

The inconsistencies between the preface and the novel are shown even more clearly in the two key moments of the preface – the narrator's discovery of the scarlet letter and his subsequent theory of imagination by moonlight. For in these moments, what elsewhere appeared mere inconsistency becomes more clearly an intentional self-contradiction – Hawthorne's means of standing behind his fictionalized persona to deny by counterexample the theory of the romantic imagination expounded. The first scene is the simpler one. On an "idle" day, the Surveyor narrator retreats to the "second story" of the Custom-House to revive his "fancy" by poking around in old documents. Here he finds a parchment commission in which are wrapped documents "not official, but of a private nature" and "a small roll of dingy paper" tied together with a "certain affair of fine red cloth" (pp. 30–1).

Perhaps the very elaborateness of the scene painting is enough to make us doubt its veracity. Certainly the narrator's insistence on the authenticity of his discovery seems wearisome to modern readers, and many readers have found the narrator's measuring of the letter downright comic. At the very least, his admission that in "dressing up" his tale (the pun is significant) he has exercised as much license as if the facts were entirely imaginary effectively undercuts the factuality of the narration (p. 33). More important, even the spiritual truthfulness he claims for the scene is suspect. The narrator sees in the cloth "some deep meaning . . . most worthy of interpretation, and which, as it were, streamed forth from the mystic symbol, subtly communicating itself to my sensibilities, but evading the analysis of my mind" (p. 31). His sense of this spiritual significance is strengthened when, touching the cloth to his breast, he feels "a sensation not altogether physical, yet almost so, as of burning heat" (p. 32).

We must not let the quaintness of this famous moment go unmarked as merely "the kind of thing they liked better back then."

The extravagance of the scene would have been obvious even in the nineteenth century. Moreover, the narrator himself unwittingly questions the validity of his response later in the novel. At the dramatic climax of the forest scene, just after Hester flings off the letter, the narrator imagines (hypothetically) that the letter will lie on the bank "like a lost jewel, which some ill-fated wanderer might pick up, and thenceforth be haunted by strange phantoms of guilt, sinkings of the heart, and unaccountable misfortune" (p. 202). The aside is striking enough in the damage it does to the narrative impetus. Even more amazing, however, is the projected history of guilt, heart sinking, and unaccountable misfortune for anyone who would pick it up. Such gothicism, a miscalculation from any author, is unconscionable in this particular narrator, the one person who supposedly has firsthand knowledge of what really happens when one holds the cloth. And the clear contradiction between his two accounts of touching the letter seriously undermines the reliability of both.[24]

More subtle but equally undeniable antinomies inform the theory of the Romantic imagination in the famous scene by moonlight. The passage directly follows the attic scene as a commentary and is central both to the narrator's specific sense of the Custom-House's effect on his imagination and to Hawthorne's more general distinction between the romance and the novel.

> Moonlight, in a familiar room, falling so white upon the carpet, and showing all its figures so distinctly, – making every object so minutely visible, yet so unlike a morning or noontide visibility, – is a medium the most suitable for a romance-writer to get acquainted with his illusive guests. There is the little domestic scenery of the well-known apartment; the chairs, with each its separate individuality; the centre-table, sustaining a work-basket, a volume or two, and an extinguished lamp; the sofa; the book-case; the picture on the wall, – all these details, so completely seen, are so spiritualized by the unusual light, that they seem to lose their actual substance, and become things of intellect. Nothing is too small or too trifling to undergo this change, and acquire dignity thereby. A child's shoe; the doll, seated in her little wicker carriage; the hobby-horse; – whatever, in a word, has been used or played with, during the day, is now invested with a quality of strangeness and remoteness, though still almost as vividly present as by daylight. (pp. 35–6)

This famous set piece is compelling. Yet, in terms of its relation to the "Custom-House" essay as a whole, one is tempted to ask what all the fuss is about and why the narrator feels his imagination is insufficient.[25] The passage comes after two different but perfectly acceptable imaginative re-creations of the past – the descriptions of the Old General and Surveyor Pue. Moreover, it is followed – as we have seen – by the admission that the real project may not be romance but the transcription of the commonplace, for which not moonlight but "insight" and "cunning" are the necessary ingredients. Even without these comparisons, the passage may undercut the theory in its very choice of language. What the narrator seeks in moonlight is not the truly creative and imaginative, but only a "delicate harvest of fancy and sensibility." And the movement of the section tends to qualify its initial terms. The spiritualizing power of the moon is redefined as "cold spirituality," the warming coal as the too clinical "half-extinguished anthracite." And most strikingly, the "moonlight" that begins the paragraph is dismissed by the end as mere "moonshine."

But, as with the discovery scene, the real problem is that the implications of the moonlight scene are undermined by the novel itself. The narrator's basic point – both here and in the definition of his artistic project immediately afterward – is that the material and actual must be rendered "strange" and "remote" by various defamiliarizing techniques, of which moonlight is the most literal and the "imaginative faculty" the most figurative. Yet, in fact, moonlight and defamiliarization are not treated positively when they reappear – explicitly echoing the "Custom-House" formulations – in the novel. In "The Minister's Vigil," the narrator remains curiously neutral on the truthfulness of the midnight vision. The light of the meteor is said to show "the familiar scene of the street, with the distinctness of midday, but also with the awfulness that is always imparted to familiar objects by an unaccustomed light. . . . all were visible, but with a singularity of aspect that seemed to give another moral interpretation to the things of this world than they had ever borne before" (p. 154). The "singularity of aspect" does not necessarily mark this "noon of that strange and solemn splendor" as good or its moral true; and at the very least, the moment stands in sharp contrast to the real "distinctness" of the midday sun under which Dimmesdale makes his final confession (p. 254).

The scene in fact is linguistically closer not to the final "revelation" but to Dimmesdale's wandering "in a maze" when leaving the forest. Here too confronted with the "unaccustomed," he "took an impression of change from the series of familiar objects that presented themselves" (p. 216). As the narrator makes increasingly clear, these "impressions" — of his church "so very strange, and yet so familiar" and later the "same perception of strangeness" in his "accustomed" study — are simply misleading, the products of his "bedazzled eyes" (pp. 217, 222, 225). In one of the few comic moments in the generally somber novel, the narrator reduces Dimmesdale's vision of his own depravity to the desire to teach children some "very" wicked words, "good, round, solid, satisfactory, and heaven-defying oaths" (p. 220). Yet the very success of this attack on Dimmesdale tells against the narrator's own Romantic project. By describing both the midnight vigil and the bedazzled walk in terms of concepts associated with the moonlit chamber and defamiliarization, he effectively questions the validity of the concept itself. If the perception of strangeness in the familiar marks in Dimmesdale a self-dramatizing Byronism, then perhaps the strange and remote objects in the room are signs of an equally pretentious pseudo-Romantic fancy.[26]

3

The narrator's unreliability must not be overstated. Finally, he is not a fully dramatized character, like Coverdale in the later novel *The Blithedale Romance*. It is difficult at times to isolate his voice — to distinguish between his analyses and his third-person paraphrases of the characters' thoughts.[27] And in terms of what is usually meant by narrative unreliability, *The Scarlet Letter* is not really "narrated" at all. But if the novel lacks a consistent narrative voice, it has a more general narrative context — a mix of the characters' interpretations and the narrator's own. And the recognition that this context is problematic – that its conclusions are not necessarily authoritative – may help clarify the central focus of this intellectually diffuse novel.

First, the narrative unreliability frees us from having to attend too closely to the narrator's moral judgments. Although *The Scarlet Letter* has always seemed in some sense a novel of moral growth, most readers in fact have trouble charting clearly the development.[28] While Dimmesdale may grow in courage, finally discovering the willpower to confess, he does not grow in understanding, but only comes to terms with a hypocrisy he has known to be sinful from the first. Similarly, although Hester's situation in the community is constantly shifting, her relation to her act remains stable (or at least equally ambiguous) throughout, and the narrator describes her final return to Boston in the same language of penitence and sorrow so troublesome earlier in the novel.[29] But most simply, the narrator's own morals seem fatuous and even parodic: " 'Be true! Be true! Be true! Show freely to the world, if not your worst, yet some trait whereby the worst may be inferred!' " (p. 260). Whatever we think of this reading of Dimmesdale's hypocrisy, it is hard to trust the narrator's equation of the truest with the worst. And his faith in the power of inference seems highly suspect in this novel of ambiguity and multiple readings, where virtually anything can mean anything.

The ambiguous status of the narrative's moralizing forces us to look elsewhere for a thematic center. In a work in which all interpretations are problematic, prescriptive morality begins to seem merely one more example of faulty epistemology, and the book's true focus less the nature of sin than of language itself. Whatever we think of the main characters' relation to their moral dilemmas, it is at least clear that all have similar problems with the meaning of symbols, a difficulty shared more generally by the narrator.[30] Not only does the significance of Hester's letter change during the course of the novel. The narrator's language itself does not seem an accurate vehicle of communication, and his conflation of seventeenth- and nineteenth-century rhetorics is finally only a special case of his more general linguistic imprecision. Everywhere Hawthorne works to problematize the text – and not always for reasons of greater psychological realism. Even the celebrated struc-

70

tural perfection of the novel is merely apparent. As Hester herself realizes, the climactic forest scene does not really change the characters' philosophical assumptions. And of course, Hawthorne willfully destroys the symmetry of the novel proper by attaching the unwieldy "Custom-House" as preface.

More generally, Hawthorne peppers his apparently serious narrative with a series of puns, whose humor seems largely to escape the narrator. Most obvious are the nasty sexual puns. The narrator repeatedly comments on how people stare at Hester's breasts, without ever sensing that moral indignation may in this case mask a far more fundamental lechery.[31] Nor does he seem to understand the complex of art puns, whereby the language of craft and design characterizes both Hester's embroidery and the magistrates' plots to control her.[32] Most strikingly, the narrator seems not to notice his repeated use of forms of the loaded word "custom" in both the essay and the novel to describe the habitual and the everyday as well as the socialized and regulated.[33]

The narrator's failure to control his language seems part of the general problem of interpretation in the book. Perhaps narrative ambiguity can be read as Hawthorne's accustomed tone. The three reasons why Hester stays in Boston and the four explanations of the mark on Dimmesdale's chest recall similarly ambivalent explanations of Goodman Brown's night or of Mr. Hooper's sin. And, here as there, such multiple readings demonstrate the irrelevance of the questions asked. No amount of precision about what Brown sees in the forest can determine what he should conclude from such spectral evidence.[34] So, no amount of clarity about what was actually on Dimmesdale's chest can indicate what its presence means – let alone address the more important issue of whether his revelation of the mark is sincere or one more form of subtle hypocrisy.[35] Yet at times this ambiguity becomes virtually self-parodic, and suggests less the difficulty of answering the specific question than the impossibility of ever saying anything precisely. Wondering what plea could be offered if Dimmesdale were to fall again in the woods, the narrator – in a long sentence fragment – follows his immediate response of "None" with a string of six answers, each longer and syntactically more convoluted than the one before (pp. 200–1). The ease with which motives can be generated does not clarify Dimmesdale's particular psychological situation, but merely challenges the whole project of interpreting motives.

Moreover, this inscrutability does not mark the complexity of human motives but is a general characteristic of all texts, as the novel emphasizes in a complex of metaphors and puns linking people and books. The beadle's cry of "open a passage" that allows Hester to enter the square (and the story) is as literary and biblical as it is literal (p. 54). The submerged hermeneutical pun is made explicit shortly afterward in Chillingworth's recognition of the Puritans' judgment as a wise "sentence," one that will make Hester a "living sermon" (p. 63).[36] Dimmesdale himself admits the equivalence of letter and world when, at the end of his "maze," he sees with bedazzled eyes his sermon as a "vast, unmeasurable tract of unwritten space" (p. 225). And, as if to summarize these bewildering continuities, the novel punningly concludes with a hypothetical "motto" to the novel as "legend," the heraldic "wording" of a picture of the red letter on the "engraved" tombstone (p. 264).

It is not enough, however, to remark the language's ironic undermining of its own assertions. For although the novel challenges some of its own most basic assumptions, it does so within a general context of certainty: However much we suspect the narrator's judgment, there is no reason to doubt the accuracy of his facts or descriptions. And although linguistic indeterminacy is surely a central issue, the book is less a general celebration of the glories of deconstruction than a specific attack on the excesses of reception theory, the problem of reader-responding to the alphabet. The narrative's inability to determine the meaning of specific phenomena raises the more basic question of what it means for something to have a meaning in the first place. This is, of course, a novel in which things appear meaningful. The letter's significance may not be clear, or even stable; but that it is significant is not questioned, any more by Hester or the narrator than by the Puritan magistrates.

Yet there is, submerged in the novel, a voice that denies such interpretations altogether – that of Chillingworth. Although not reliable as a moral exemplar, Chillingworth in his nominalism (as in his materialism) offers a healthy corrective to the overreading everywhere else in the narrative. Early he tells Hester that he wishes her to live " 'so that this burning shame may still blaze upon thy bosom' " (p. 73). Although hardly charitable, the comment is refreshingly untainted by the general tendency to turn Hester's letter (and her breasts) into signifiers. For Chillingworth, the letter is a "shame" — the mark of public disapprobation — but not itself a sin, and her bosom is simply a place on her body.[37] He makes these implications explicit in a later conversation: " 'By thy first step awry, thou didst plant the germ of evil; but, since that moment, it has all been a dark necessity. Ye that have wronged me are not sinful, save in a kind of typical illusion; neither am I fiend-like, who have snatched a fiend's office from his hands. It is our fate' " (p. 174). Chillingworth is probably wrong. The belief that "fate," as a "dark necessity," excuses responsibility is highly suspect, leading as it does to the refusal of redemption by which the proud traditionally ensure their damnation.[38] Yet his notion of a "typical illusion" — of typology as illusory in its tendency to redefine "wrongs" as "sins" — seems more accurate than Hester's need to allegorize the situation as the characters' " 'wandering together in this gloomy maze of evil' " (p. 174).

Yet the real mark of the book's antisymbolism — or at least of its wariness over the ease with which things are made to signify — is Pearl. Pearl has traditionally been something of a problem to readers, and to many she seems the most exclusively allegorical of the characters.[39] She is certainly treated as such by all in the novel, including the narrator himself. But again, this interpretation may be less Hawthorne's than part of the general tendency he criticizes. That many of the acts that supposedly define Pearl's allegorical character derive from Hawthorne's description of his daughter should itself qualify their significance: Surely Una did not "symbolize" anything to her father, and her wildness was merely healthy animality, not a mark of her demonic origin.[40] Even Pearl's most allegorical actions admit of a naturalistic interpretation: Her fixation on Hester's letter or the minister's covering his heart with his hand may simply mark a child's natural fascination with the unusual, or may even be a meaningless reflection of what she unconsciously perceives as the adult world's more conscious preoccupation with the signs. Moreover, some of her actions —

most notably (and comically) her pelting pigeons with pebbles during Hester's second meeting with Chillingworth – resist even the narrator's talent for allegorization (p. 177). And whether or not her symbolic "errand as a messenger of anguish" is fulfilled in Dimmesdale's deathbed confession, it is the legacy of the anti-typological Chillingworth that permits her literal escape from Boston.

But most important, the narrator and characters undercut and deny their own allegorization even as they indulge in it. The narrator is, for the most part, careful to present all readings of Pearl's hieroglyphic dimension as projections of the characters. On those occasions when the narrator himself indulges in such symbolic readings – such as the legend of Pearl's taming the forest beasts – he explicitly calls attention to the "improbable" nature of the account (pp. 204–5). Moreover, the characters themselves criticize their tendency to read Pearl as allegory. Not only the narrator, but the elders as well, question the wisdom of Hester's dressing Pearl symbolically in red. Although he accepts the appropriateness of the costume when he learns who Pearl is, Mr. Wilson's first and more natural response is to object to such symbolism: " 'what has ailed thy mother to bedizen thee in this strange fashion?' " (p. 110). Wilson probably objects only to the strangeness of this particular costume, but it is hard not to read through his reaction to question the wisdom of any fashion – whether dress or letter – that pretends to illustrate the essential being of the wearer.

Pearl, then, is not so much a symbol of guilt and sin as a measure of the consequences of a certain kind of interpretation – a perfectly realistic picture of the psychological trauma resulting when a child is dressed as a symbol and her eyeballs are scrutinized for images of the devil. So, more generally, whatever the moral implications of Hawthorne's characterizations, their psychological precision undermines the validity of any symbolic reading. We tend to assume that Dimmesdale avoids Pearl less because she symbolizes his shame than because he fears that others will see in her the physical marks of his paternity. But our very preference for psychology over typology implicitly denies the value of reading Pearl allegorically. Thus, in one sense, Dimmesdale's cowardly relation to Pearl is more consistent than the others', even more than the narrator's and our own, for he at least senses (as we do not always) that Pearl is more nearly the result of his semen than of his sin. One might almost say that psychological realism throughout the novel exposes Puritan moralism as a species of faulty semantics: that whether or not Dimmesdale's hypocrisy reveals his own unregenerateness, it suggests the inadequacy of the Puritans' mode of interpretation – typology as a kind of sublimation.

4

Once the authority of the novel's narration is challenged, the book's moralism, its symbolism, and even its psychological subtlety are seen to share in a more basic (and problematic) theory of knowledge and meaning. And what at first seemed intellectually confused becomes a telling dramatization of a confusion about the limits of intellect. Yet even though Hawthorne's point of view is clear, the novel's historical trappings seem too precise for his target to be merely the general limitations of meaning and allegory. The conflation of two historically localized vocabularies does not prove the indeterminacy of all vocabularies, any more than Champollion is best glossed as the forerunner of Wittgenstein. Even Hawthorne's characterization of Pearl's resistance to allegorization is historically determined, presupposing certain assumptions about the meaningfulness of children not common to all cultures and contexts. The question that remains, then, is why linguistic indeterminacy is presented in terms of this particular setting.

Here the clue may lie with one of the text's most peculiar preoccupations: its fascination with birthmarks as impressions of the mind on the body. We have already noted Hester's search in Pearl for the physical and spiritual signs of her own overactive imagination. But there are other, more unusual allusions – many employing this loaded terminology of "impressions" and "influences." Sir Kenelm Digby, the man Hawthorne associates most closely with the Renaissance interest in birthmarks, for example, is explicitly singled out as one of Chillingworth's teachers (p. 121). And, of course, the crowd's interpretation of Dimmesdale's **A** as the physical result of his mental torment implies a similar model of mind–body exchange.[41]

Hawthorne is not merely indulging in a little intellectual local color. The preoccupation with birthmarks, as we have seen, actually came somewhat later in the century; and Digby himself is less important in the seventeenth century than in the nineteenth century's rediscovery of it. Whatever its real significance, Digby's interest in birthmarks seemed in the nineteenth century to anticipate contemporary scientific experiments in its delineation of the continuity between the natural and spiritual worlds. In a famous passage near the end of *Nature,* Emerson lists as examples of spirituality not only Christ's miracles and more recent political and religious revolutions, including that of Swedenborg; he even includes "many obscure and yet contested facts, now arranged under the name of Animal Magnetism; prayers; eloquence; self-healing; and the wisdom of children" (CW, vol. I, p. 43). The negative consequences of such jumbling of the spiritual and the pseudo-scientific — and Digby's part in them — are clearer in Oliver Wendell Holmes's account of the age's "delusions." In attacking the fashionable homeopathic belief that like cures like, Holmes gives a brief history of all such false enthusiasms, tracing them back to their origins in seventeenth-century theories of weapon salves popularized by Francis Bacon and especially Digby.[42]

Holmes objects primarily to the inflated claims and inadequate evidence of the pseudoscientists. Hawthorne, however, focuses more on the theoretical implications. Warning his fiancée against seeking in mesmerism a cure for her headaches, he is less worried that hypnotism is a fraud than that it is not. "Supposing that this power [of the mesmerist over his patient] arises from the transfusion of one spirit into another, it seems to me that the sacredness of the individual is violated by it; there would be an intrusion into thy holy of holies — and the intruder would not be thy husband!"

But the problem is not simply that of the unpardonable sin as a kind of spiritual rape. For mesmerism does more than violate the individual; it degrades the whole notion of the spiritual.

> Without distrusting that the phenomena which thou tellest me of, and others as remarkable, have really occurred, I think that they are to be accounted for as the result of a physical and material, not of a spiritual, influence. . . . And what delusion can be more lamentable and mischievous, than to mistake the physical and material for the

76

spiritual? What so miserable as to lose the soul's true, though hidden, knowledge and consciousness of heaven, in the mist of an earth-born vision?[43]

And, as Coverdale argues in a passage closely echoing Hawthorne's own thoughts, the most likely result will be to sacrifice true spirituality (even heaven) in the pursuit of a spurious variety.

If these phenomena have not humbug at the bottom, so much the worse for us. What can they indicate, in a spiritual way, except that the soul of man is descending to a lower point than it has ever before reached, while incarnate? We are pursuing a downward course, in the eternal march, and thus bring ourselves into the same range with beings whom death, in requital of their gross and evil lives, has degraded below humanity. To hold intercourse with spirits of this order, we must stoop, and grovel in some element more vile than earthly dust. These goblins, if they exist at all, are but the shadows of past mortality, outcasts, mere refuse-stuff, adjudged unworthy of the eternal world, and, on the most favorable supposition, dwindling gradually into nothingness. The less we have to say to them, the better; lest we share their fate! (Vol. III, p. 199)

The allusions to Digby, the alchemists, and even modern pseudosciences like phrenology and physiognomy associate the intellectual action of the novel with this disastrous conflation of the material and the spiritual. Witchcraft − present throughout the book, especially in the figure of Mistress Hibbins − is the most obvious such conflation, equating as it does verbal formulas and physical recipes with demonic influences. But as the characterization of Chillingworth implies, witchcraft is only an idiosyncratic version of the mistake made by all pseudoscientists, perhaps by all scientists. In those days in which natural learning was felt to be a substitute for "religious zeal," "it may be that the higher and more subtle faculties of such men [as Chillingworth] were materialized, and that they lost the spiritual view of existence amid the intricacies of that wondrous mechanism, which seemed to involve art enough to comprise all of life within itself" (p. 119). These "scientific attainments . . . hardly less than supernatural," like sorcery itself, are suspect not because they are hysteria and credulity masquerading as knowledge. More importantly, as Coverdale realizes, they are founded on and perpetuate a debased model of the soul. Thus, Chillingworth's sin is not some generalized violation of

Dimmesdale's privacy, but a materialization that implicitly denies all spirituality. His scientific credo – the belief that "a bodily disease, which we look upon as whole and entire within itself, may, after all, be but a symptom of some ailment in the spiritual part" (p. 136) – although apparently accepting the primacy of spirit, actually traps it in a medical, material metaphor. And his power over the minister rests less with the psychological effects of his prying than with the metaphysical implications of his theory.

Yet Chillingworth is not unaided in his covert attack on the spirit. For although his materialism corrupts Dimmesdale, the minister is a willing accomplice. Perhaps the Puritans' notion of the visibility of sanctity is already dangerously physical; surely Dimmesdale's own search for "symptoms" of sin betrays a subtly materialist approach to the spirit.[44] Moreover – we are told – Dimmesdale's class of divines, the nonpentecostal spiritualists, were "etherealized . . . by spiritual communications with the better world," and Dimmesdale's own "ethereal attributes," which might have spoken to angels, are "kept down" by his "burden, whatever it might be, of crime or anguish" (pp. 141, 142). Although the narrator seems to present these descriptions neutrally, it is impossible to read them so in light of Hawthorne's reservations about spiritual communications. The key word here is "etherealized." To modern ears a neutral term implying "unearthly," through the nineteenth century the term referred more precisely to the notion of an "ether," posited specifically by cosmologists and more generally by other philosophers to bridge the gap between pure matter and pure soul.[45] It is this concept of the ethereal as an interface – or "medium," the novel's preferred term, borrowed like the others from contemporary discussions – that was ridiculed by Emerson as "matter reduced to an extreme thinness" and by Holmes as the "vague belief that matter subdivided grows less material, and approaches nearer to a spiritual nature as it requires a more powerful telescope for its detection."[46]

The ambiguities of this whole concept of spirit are epitomized in the climactic paragraph describing the "interior" of Dimmesdale's heart.

> None of these visions ever quite deluded him. At any moment, by an effort of his will, he could discern substances through their misty

lack of substance, and convince himself that they were not solid in their nature, like yonder table of carved oak, or that big, square, leathern-bound and brazen-clasped volume of divinity. But, for all that, they were, in one sense, the truest and most substantial things which the poor minister now dealt with. It is the unspeakable misery of a life so false as his, that it steals the pith and substance out of whatever realities there are around us, and which were meant by Heaven to be the spirit's joy and nutriment. To the untrue man, the whole universe is false, – it is impalpable, – it shrinks to nothing within his grasp. And he himself, in so far as he shows himself in a false light, becomes a shadow, or, indeed, ceases to exist. The only truth, that continued to give Mr. Dimmesdale a real existence on this earth, was the anguish in his inmost soul, and the undissembled expression of it in his aspect. (pp. 145–6)

In trying to overcome various visions – including those of "ethereal" angels – Dimmesdale insists on the solidity of commonplace objects in one more of the novel's denials of the preface's project of defamiliarization. Nevertheless, the narrator tells us, Dimmesdale's hypocrisy steals the substance out of the realities Heaven intends to be the spirit's nutriment, leaving visions as the only true substances.

The narrator's analysis, however, may not be authoritative. It assumes too uncritically the very continuity (and even cannibalism) between spirit and matter that other sections question.[47] The definition of the "untrue man" and his world is highly problematic, echoing equally troublesome moments in Emerson. The shrinkage of the world to nothing is one more "vanishing," similar to the moment in the Divinity School "Address" when, after man's discovery of the omnipresence of law, "then shrinks the great world at once into a mere illustration and fable of [his] mind" (CW, vol. I, p. 76). So Dimmesdale's belief in himself as a shadow, really existing only in his anguish, recalls the moment in "The Christmas Banquet" when Gervayse Hastings finds his own shadowiness in his inability to grieve; and, behind both passages, Emerson's lament over Waldo's death in "Experience."[48] But most simply, given the novel's distrust in signs and birthmarks, it is unclear whether the "anguish in his universal soul" and the "undissembled expression" of it in his face are in fact Dimmesdale's "only truth" or the false notion of an "ethereal" continuity that creates the problem in the first place.

Hawthorne's criticism may in fact be even more precise – and more historically determined – in its repeated (even obsessive) association of this confused notion of spirit with the concept of sympathy.[49] "Sympathy," of course, is a very broad term, with an important place in Romantic theories of the imagination and, behind that, eighteenth-century sentimentalist ethics.[50] But these modern references to some general sort of fellow feeling derive from an older Renaissance explanation of the relation between mind and body. By this account, the physical resemblance between the atoms of the mind or imagination and those of external objects results in a series of apparently spiritual but actually mechanical continuities, analogous to the "sympathetic" vibrations of two harp strings. The concept is central to the alchemists' insistence on the importance of the psychological state of the experimenter, and is present in most early scientific literature, especially that of Paracelsus and Francis Bacon.

The theory finds its fullest explanation, however, in Digby's treatise "Of the Sympathetick Powder." To explain how a bloody cloth soaked in a solution of the powder could cure a wound over great distance, Digby postulated that atoms of blood evaporate into the air and eventually circulate back to their proper home in the wound, carrying with them the "sticky" atoms of healing powder. The theoretical basis of his explanation is that "in the actions of all our senses, there is a material and corporal participation of the things we are sensible of, *viz.* some atoms of the body operate upon our Senses, and enter into their organs; which serve them as funnels, to conduct and carry them to the brain and the imagination."[51]

Hawthorne's use of the term "sympathy," of course, embraces all its meanings – Romantic, ethical, and scientific. What is interesting, however, is that the last – this quirky definition of a mechanical exchange between world and brain – is, if anything, the most frequent. In an early use of the term, Chillingworth tells Hester, " 'I come to the inquest with other senses than [the magistrates] possess. I shall seek this man, as I have sought truth in books; as I have sought gold in alchemy. There is a sympathy that will make me conscious of him. I shall see him tremble. I shall feel myself shudder, suddenly and unawares'" (p. 75). The mate-rialistic bias of his explanation should not be taken lightly. Sympathy is indeed a "sense" and the model of operation atomistic, quite literally like Chillingworth's alchemical attempts to transform lead into gold. And his "shudder" marks less his emotional reaction to the sin than the extent to which all theories of sympathy depend on a literal, even molecular, vibration. So later, the characterization of Hester's "sympathetic throb" as an "electric thrill" or of Dimmesdale's sympathies with the sinful as moments when his heart "vibrated in unison" with theirs emphasizes the mechanistic origins of the concept (pp. 87, 142; cf. p. 67).

More generally, this implicit materialism recalls the extent to which, even when not explicitly attacked as pseudospiritual, sympathy in this novel may not be positive. Many readers have noted that, although theoretically the sympathetic should react equally to virtue and vice, characters in fact "sympathize" more fully with evil. Dimmesdale's "sympathy and fellowship" with the wicked while wandering in his maze in part records one more aspect of his bedazzlement (p. 222). Yet the very redundancy suggests that the proof may in fact work more the other way – less to show his fancied sympathy as one more confusion than to imply that sympathy as a concept may itself be inherently confused. A similarly dual focus informs the famous passage earlier in which Hester "imagines" and "fancies" that her letter gives her "a sympathetic knowledge of the hidden sin in other hearts" (p. 86). The obvious criticism is of Hester's tendency, like those of Roderick and other Hawthorne characters, to turn her sin into pride, an inverted mark of her uniqueness.[52] But this error results as much from epistemological presuppositions as from psychological weaknesses. It is not simply that people tend to recast their flaws as strengths: The very notion of "sympathetic knowledge" as a "new sense" – something physical that nevertheless reveals the spiritual – encourages them to misread natural events as the signs of spiritual truths.

The dangerous tendencies of sympathy as a concept are most evident, however, not in the seventeenth-century characters but in the most consistently Romantic voice in the novel – that of the narrator himself. And its failure as a psychological principle is clearest in the most blatantly symbolic aspect of the book – the famously compliant sun in the forest scene. It is hard to take seriously the overstated light imagery of these chapters – from Hester's initial characterization of the sun as Pearl's follow spot to the sunshine's flickering on and off in response to the lovers' reviving sexual interest. Moreover, the language of the passage virtually insists that we question the interpretation.

> And, as if the gloom of the earth and sky had been but the effluence of these two mortal hearts, it vanished with their sorrow. All at once, as with a sudden smile of heaven, forth burst the sunshine, pouring a very flood into the obscure forest, gladdening each green leaf, transmuting the yellow fallen ones to gold, and gleaming adown the gray trunks of the solemn trees. (pp. 202–3)

The syntax may seem unnecessarily hypothetical, and the mixed metaphor "flood of sunshine" to imply a dangerous conflation, at least of light and love. But more simply, the familiar Emersonian terms "vanish" and "gladden" clearly place the description in a suspect Romantic tradition, as does the "joy" that ends the paragraph. And the unexpected 'reference to alchemy – the light's "transmutation" of yellow to "gold" – recalls the degree to which such allusions work earlier to discredit the interpretation.

The narrator's conclusion, the most extended praise of Romantic sympathy in the novel, is also the least convincing.

> Such was the sympathy of Nature – that wild, heathen Nature of the forest, never subjugated by human law, nor illumined by higher truth – with the bliss of these two spirits! Love, whether newly born, or aroused from a deathlike slumber, must always create a sunshine, filling the heart so full of radiance, that it overflows upon the outward world. Had the forest still kept its gloom, it would have been bright in Hester's eyes, and bright in Arthur Dimmesdale's! (p. 203)

The logic, of course, does not work. The attempt to defend the lovers' wildness by citing nature's sympathy is undermined by the final implication that the light may reside not in the world but in the lovers' perception of it. The claim is not quite Emerson's famous insistence that "an act of truth or heroism seems at once to draw to itself the sky as its temple, the sun as its candle" (although echoes of this and other formulations from the "Beauty" chapter of *Nature* do permeate the scene).[53] Instead of Emersonian parallelism or correspondences, the narrator argues more desperately that love "must always" create a sunshine. And the model of an imaginative "overflow" from the heart to the world seems as subtly materialistic as do earlier theories of sympathy, reducing the sun to a kind of natural birthmark created by the lovers' mental preoccupations.

The narrator's theory of sympathy, however, does not merely inform his historical narrative. It underwrites his theory of romance and the imagination in the introductory "Custom-House." The materialistic implications of the term itself are as apparent in this preface as in the novel. The "perfect sympathy" he hopes to feel with his true readers results, as we said, from the Aristophanic subdivision of one body into two (p. 3). Similarly, the "mere sensuous sympathy of dust for dust" reveals less the limitation of a certain kind of attachment than the extent to which all sympathy is "sensuous," even mechanical (p. 9). The more general moments of sympathetic identification in the essay fail to counteract this implicit materialism. In light of the alchemical origins of sympathy, it is hard to ignore the similarities between the narrator's description of the burning letter and Digby's account of the blood-soaked bandage. Similarly, the project of defamiliarization seems altogether too mechanical – a neo-Digbean recipe for "spiritualizing" objects by making them vibrate in moonlight. And both the concept of literature as "airy matter" and the more celebrated notion of a neutral territory where the actual and imaginary can intermingle recall a little too precisely the hybrid ether. [54]

5

It might seem perverse to argue that in *The Scarlet Letter* Hawthorne attacks the genial concept of sympathy, or to reduce the moral and psychological complexities of the novel to a history of closet materialism. Yet it is important to attend to the philosophical assumptions of the narrative. By using the same language to characterize the Puritans' typology, Hester's antinomianism, Dimmesdale's hypocrisy, and the narrator's Romanticism, Hawthorne suggests that in some respects they all commit the same kind of interpretive error. Moreover, through the repeated use of unusual code words – "sympathy," "medium," "impression," "influence," and terms specifically associated with medicine and animal magnetism – he situates this error within the historical tradition of pseudospiritual materialism. In part, his point is simply that we lack a truly independent vocabulary of spirit, that all language that attempts to talk about the immaterial only does so metaphorically in words drawn from (and perhaps corrupted by) the material.

Yet, this crude limitation of materialist vocabulary actually masks a more fundamental problem. By collapsing everything together, Hawthorne challenges not only our spiritual terminology but also the fundamental mind–body dichotomy that underwrites it. The Puritans, Hester, Dimmesdale, and the narrator all, in their different ways, pursue essences – the truth behind the appearance, the meaning behind the signs. Yet Hawthorne suggests that this whole notion of fundamentalism – of inmost Mes and lives within life – may be spurious, not true essentialism but only partialism with delusions of grandeur. In terms of the medical metaphor, so long as symptom and disease are seen as ontologically equivalent and equally "material," there is no problem. But repeatedly the characters interpret disease universally, making it seem more "spiritual" than its own symptoms. The result is a concept like sympathy, in which rapidly vibrating atoms are somehow equated with fellowship and good will. Hawthorne's response is simply to deny the whole explanation, to insist that sympathy is not so much a bad thing as it is not a thing at all.

The discovery of universal materialism is thus, in this more general sense, the denial of what masquerades as "immaterial." Hawthorne's target is not so much real materialism as a false objectivization of the ineffable, what we have come to call the reification of the mental: the treatment of minds, souls, and thoughts (vague concepts though they be) as if they were real objects that we understand as we understand tables. As Dimmesdale implicitly realizes, the true sin in Boston may be less sex or typology than idolatry – not the misidentification of the object but the treatment of the "inner" as an object, something that can be worshipped as an idol (p. 191). In its tendency to idolatry, visible sanctity is no better than hypocrisy; and Dimmesdale's belief that his secret self is not his visible self, only an inevitable consequence of Puritanism's belief that there is such a thing as a secret self in the first place. Moreover, both visible sanctity and hypocrisy are versions of birthmark theory: joy (or shame) in the recognition that one's mental preoccupations do (or do not) show in one's face.[55] In this respect, Transcendental rhetoric does belong in Puritan Boston, for in this error, Emerson is as fully implicated as Cotton and Swedenborg. Not only is the novel's language about Mes and lives within life explicitly Emersonian. More generally, it is he, in his seminal declaration of American literary independence, who discovers that thought can be treated as a thing. And for Hawthorne, Emerson's collapse of the thought–act dichotomy into thought-as-action – the hypostatized "American Scholar" or "Man Thinking" – is exactly the disastrous corporealization that lies at the heart of the materialization of the spiritual.

It is in terms of this reification error, then, that we must understand the problem with meaning in the book. Most simply, Hawthorne does not see the interpretive shift from Puritan typology to Transcendentalist symbolism as an improvement, or even a change. Puritan and Transcendentalist alike are committed to a dangerously mechanistic model of the continuity between world and mind, body and soul: The narrator's sun and the Puritans' stars speak the same pseudospiritual materialism. Nor is his objection merely the Emersonian one that typology and symbolism too quickly rigidify into static spiritual lexicons. Cotton may at times be indistinguishable from Swedenborg, but the solution is not for Hawthorne – as it was for Emerson – a more fluid, modernist use of symbols. For the issue is less stasis than what the fluidity of language implies – that words, like things, exist in time and change over time. Not only Hester's A but "fashion," "talent," and the ubiquitous "sympathy" itself have different meanings in different centuries. It is part of the wit of the novel to exploit that "material" or historical quality of words. And the ironic "engraved" letter of the novel's final sentence only highlights the extent to which signification is not a function of divine decree.

But the real "materialism" involves less the way words hook up with their meanings than the way meanings hook up with the world. Although characters frequently think differently, there is really no such thing as "revelation" in the book.[56] Even those who agree about what they see on Dimmesdale's chest are still faced with the greater problem of what such alphabetic inflammation might mean – if anything. More generally, the same dilemma informs all language in the book. Those who remember the original "decreed" meaning of Hester's A as an abbreviation for "adulteress" must still relate adultery to experience. What does this sin (or indeed any sin) say about the character of the sinner? To what extent may one undo a sin, and what is the proper mode of reformation? The differing answers to these questions, in turn, account for the changing attitudes within the novel.

The pseudospiritual language of the book, then, serves to delineate the epistemological origins of the work's moral dilemma – to claim that to the extent that spirit, words, and meaning are concepts, they are unintelligible; and to the extent that they are intelligible, they are actually material and no more ontologically significant than tables or chairs. Such a claim does not deny meaning: Although the book is skeptical about the significance of As in the sky, it is not so uncertain about Hester's adultery, or even her A. Meaning is less denied than its nature defined and delimited; and the book serves not to deconstruct all meaning but to question a specific notion of meaning as a special kind of thing. It is perhaps too much to ask whether A stands for "adultery" or "able." But if the letter does not have a meaning, it does have an "office": Throughout the novel, it notes quite effectively the fact that Hester once did something that society considered a mistake. Words exist as truly as people, and the meanings that attach to them are as reliable as the "offices" attached to people. Her adulterousness is, like Bellingham's governorship, real enough; the difficulty arises when people postulate, behind these rules and conventions, an absolute truth that underwrites them.[57] The problem, then, is less meaning than the false belief that meaning itself has a meaning. And what we have been calling the book's "materialist" approach to language is more simply its sense of language's conventionality.

The characters may come to understand the necessity of relativism: Both Hester and Dimmesdale seem finally to eschew ultimates and offer themselves up to the authority of God and everyday life in Boston. The narrator, however, fails to understand this conventionality, and this failure accounts for his "unreliability." In one sense, his autobiographical preface serves less to introduce the novel than to dramatize in a modern setting the error that the novel will teach Hester and the Puritan characters to understand. It is not merely that the preface is self-defeating in its plea for sympathy, although Hawthorne is surely aware that most readers will think *The Scarlet Letter* (or even "The Custom-House" alone) sufficient recompense for being fired from a boring job.[58] More simply, the narrator's whole project to escape conventionality is misconceived. And his Romantic account of his liberation from the Custom-House is itself the sin that leaves Hester and her bastard child on the scaffold.

The narrator's initial claim to preserve his inmost Me sets up the very dialectic between substance and essence that the rest of the book works to deconstruct.[59] There is of course nothing wrong with the narrator's saying – as Hawthorne himself does elsewhere – that he holds some things back. Or even with recognizing the Shandian impossibility of an absolutely complete autobiography. But the narrator insists on reading these personal and linguistic limitations as if they had ontological significance: as if what is held back were not merely additional information but some kernel of truth, the very essence of self. In this insistence, he outdoes Dimmesdale, and his exultation in withholding his inmost Me is really hypocrisy without shame.

As the narrator is the novel's real hypocrite, so is he its most radical antinomian. For the true lawlessness is not Hester's momentary belief in the self-consecration of her sin or that the world's law is no law for her mind, but the narrator's claim at the end of the essay to have become "a citizen of somewhere else" (pp. 44, 164, 195). As we have seen, in rejecting the Salem bureaucracy, the narrator merely falls back upon the Transcendental rhetoric he claims to have rejected. Moreover, although seeking in literature a neutral territory of airy matter and spiritualized burdens, he in fact remains wholly within time and space, writing only history – whether of contemporary politics or Puritan epistemologies. But most important, it is intellectually incoherent to claim to be "somewhere else." Reality and meaning are indeed eternally elusive. But even deconstruction realizes that one cannot split the *differance* – that the chief mark of deferral is man's existence on this side of it. To recognize indeterminacy and then project yourself into this indeterminate realm is logically inconsistent. The self is one of the first things to go in deconstruction's iconoclastic rampage. The process that begins by denying one's identity with the Inspector and proceeds to deny even that one is still the Surveyor can honestly end only with the denial that one is altogether.

The problem of meaning in *The Scarlet Letter*, then, is the problem – both theoretically sophisticated and historically localizable– of confusing the true materiality of language with the apparent materiality of spirit. The tendency to corporealize concepts (not to say incarnate them) has been natural since at least the time of Descartes. But negation is the inevitable result of all such reifications.[60] The only effective defense against the process is not to mystify reality through a pseudospiritual pursuit of the Actual in the unfamiliar, but to refuse altogether to describe the ineffable.[61] Whether or not life is a prison, it is something that must take place within rules and limits – the custom-houses of history, society, and language. The attempt to escape the customary simply misrepresents how life and society, even meaning and language, work. For as the labyrinthine anachronisms of the text – its fights between past and present, psychology and semantics, history and actuality – finally show, the rejection of reality is itself not imaginative, but only a disreputable local moment in the history of thought. And time, not truth, is the inevitable condition of existence.

NOTES

1 These tales share with *The Scarlet Letter* certain philosophical assumptions. There are, of course, more famous theological and historical similarities, even related plot motifs, throughout the Puritan tales, especially in "Endicott and the Red Cross."

2 On the meaning of the novel's historical errors, see Michael J. Colacurcio, "Footsteps of Ann Hutchinson: The Context of *The Scarlet Letter*," *ELH* 39 (1972): 459–94; and Michael Davitt Bell, *Hawthorne*

and the Historical Romance of New England (Princeton, N.J.: Princeton University Press, 1971), pp. 126–46. For a more traditional review of Hawthorne's use of his sources, see Charles Ryskamp, "The New England Sources of *The Scarlet Letter,*" *American Literature* 31 (1959): 257–72.

3 Although the term "hieroglyphic" had been used to mean "emblematic" since at least the seventeenth century, nineteenth-century uses clearly refer more specifically to contemporary archaeological discoveries. On the relation between Egyptology and writing, see John T. Irwin, *American Hieroglyphics: The Symbol of the Egyptian Hieroglyphics in the American Renaissance* (New Haven, Conn.: Yale University Press, 1980).

4 The most sophisticated brief introduction is Inge Jonsson, *Emanuel Swedenborg* (New York: Twayne, 1971); on correspondences, see especially pp. 104–8. A good contemporary source is Emerson's chapter on "Language" in *Nature;* in fact, much of the best Swedenborgian scholarship grows out of responses to this chapter (and to similar Swedenborgianism in Blake).

5 Like "hieroglyphic," "physiognomy" is a Renaissance term revived by the Romantics in a specific scientific context. "Phrenology" and its related terminology, on the other hand, are nineteenth-century neologisms. On "combativeness" as a phrenological term, see George Combe, *The Constitution of Man Considered in Relation to External Objects* (Boston: Carter and Hendee, 1829), p. 72. Hawthorne read this work in 1836. For a similar use of phrenological terminology to characterize Aylmer in "The Birth-mark," see vol. X, p. 36. On Hawthorne's interest in phrenology and physiognomy in general, and Combe in particular, see Taylor Stoehr, *Hawthorne's Mad Scientists: Pseudoscience and Social Science in Nineteenth-Century Life and Letters* (Hamden, Conn.: Archon, 1978).

6 "Credulity" is the term used in early pseudoscientific literature for the power of belief or faith that allows the scientist to achieve his experimental end. It is often linked with the "power of the imagination," although that concept had not yet acquired its Romantic overtones. For representative uses of the term, and its explicitly religious origins, see Cornelius Agrippa, *Three Books of Occult Philosophy*, trans. J. F. [reake] (London: printed by R. W. for Gregory Moule, 1651), pp. 149, 354; and Arthur Edward Waite, ed., *The Hermetic and Alchemical Writing of Paracelsus*, vol. II (1894; reprint Berkeley: Shambhala, 1976), p. 300. For an explicit contemporary recognition of the meaning, see Poe's marginalia on credulity in the Virginia edition of *The Complete*

Works of Edgar Allan Poe, vol. XVI, ed. James A. Harrison (New York: Thomas Y. Crowell, 1902), p. 92. Hawthorne makes a similar use of the term in "The Birth-mark," vol. X, p. 48.

7 All three terms are common throughout the novel, and indeed throughout Hawthorne. For representative uses of "gloomy," see for example pp. 43, 199, 202, 227. For "sorrow," see pp. 17, 95, 202, 263. For the more important term "morbid," frequently associated with Dimmesdale, see pp. 130, 155, 159, 178, 200, 239. For similar uses of the terms elsewhere in Hawthorne, see "The Minister's Black Veil" (vol. IX, p. 46), "Egotism" (vol. X, p. 273), and "The Christmas Banquet" (vol. X, p. 296). Michael J. Colacurcio discusses the importance of the conflation of Romantic "sorrow" and Puritan "sin" in "Parson Hooper's Power of Blackness: Sin and Self in 'The Minister's Black Veil,'" *Prospects* 5 (1980): 331–411.

8 One should at least recall the extent to which the heart in Hawthorne is negative, a foul cavern. See for example the devil's famous characterization of it in "Earth's Holocaust" (vol. X, p. 403) and the notebook passage that lies behind it (vol. VIII, p. 237).

9 For Winthrop's interest in such phenomena and his friendship with Digby, see Robert C. Black, *The Younger John Winthrop* (New York: Columbia University Press, 1966), pp. 307–19. For Cotton Mather's even more famous interest in birthmarks (and Digby), see his *The Angel of Bethesda* (Barre, Mass.: American Antiquarian Society and Barre Publishers, 1972), pp. 31, 163, 241, 246; and his letters to the Royal Society of London, summarized in their *Philosophical Transactions,* vol. XXIX (New York: Johnson Reprint Corp. and Kraus Reprint Corp., 1963), pp. 62–71. See also Kenneth Silverman, ed., *Selected Letters of Cotton Mather* (Baton Rouge: Louisiana State University Press, 1971), esp. pp. 107–22; and on Mather's science in general, Robert Middlekauff, *The Mathers: Three Generations of Puritan Intellectuals, 1596–1728* (New York: Oxford University Press, 1971), pp. 279–319.

10 For a more orthodox account of the relation between the soul and the body, see Book I, Chapter XV of John Calvin, *Institutes of the Christian Religion,* (vol. I, Philadelphia: Westminster Press, 1960), pp. 183–96. Hester's heresy is called "Traducianism," the belief that the soul is in some sense inherited from the parents rather than created in each child by God. For Calvin's rejection, see *Institutes,* vol. I, p. 191. In a general sense, of course, original sin is only the oldest and most important birthmark. Usually, however, the Puritans avoid making this equation. Although they admit that original sin produces disease, they do not see disease necessarily as a mark of original sin. Most

birthmark rhetoric focuses on questions that are entirely nonspiritual, the study of a craving for strawberries that produces a strawberry mark. Hester effectively inverts this emphasis. Although she sees her passion less as a sin than as a physical response, she nevertheless imagines that this physical state influences Pearl's psychological, spiritual nature. For a more orthodox view of the relation between birthmarks and sin, see Mather, *Angel*, pp. 31–32.

11 *The Collected Works of Ralph Waldo Emerson*, ed. Robert E. Spiller et al., vol. III (Cambridge, Mass.: Harvard University Press, 1971–), p. 43. Subsequent references to Emerson are to this edition (CW), cited parenthetically by volume and page number.

12 See p. 211; cf. CW, vol. I, p. 10. The term "infinite space" has generally had an important place in cosmological debates from Descartes to Newton about the nature of extension. For this tradition, see Alexander Koyre, *From the Closed World to the Infinite Universe* (New York: Harper & Row, 1958).

13 For representative vanishings in the novel, see pp. 57, 59, 63, 69, 92, 119, 149, 156, 166, 169, 184, 202, 260. For the famous vanishings in *Nature*, see CW, vol. I, pp. 10, 45.

14 See, for example, pp. 174, 183, 199, 245, and, of course, the title of Chapter 20. There is one use before the description of Hester's labyrinth (p. 99).

15 Hester's desire for certainty about her salvation – or at least her belief that murder would speed up God's decision – recalls famous historical instances in which damnation seemed more supportable than constant anxiety and self-scrutiny: the suicide of Edwards's uncle Hawley, for example, or the Puritan woman's throwing her baby in a well to ensure her own damnation. Dimmesdale uses a similar logic of despair to justify his intention to flee Boston (p. 201).

16 Since D. H. Lawrence, much criticism of the novel treats Hester's antinomianism as a proto-Romantic response to the repressive nature of Puritan society. For representative recent versions of this reading, see Joel Porte, *The Romance in America: Studies in Cooper, Poe, Hawthorne, Melville, and James* (Middletown, Conn.: Wesleyan University Press, 1969), pp. 98–106; and Nina Baym, *The Shape of Hawthorne's Career* (Ithaca, N.Y.: Cornell University Press, 1976), pp. 123–43.

17 Recent work on "The Custom-House" is extensive. For analyses that attend largely to the essay's internal unity, see Dan McCall, "The Design of Hawthorne's 'Custom-House,'" *Nineteenth-Century Fiction* 21 (1967): 349–58; Paul John Eakin, "Hawthorne's Imagination and the Structure of 'The Custom-House,'" *American Literature* 43 (1971):

346–58; and Baym, *Shape*, pp. 143–51. For readings that focus largely on the essay's relation to the novel, see Larzer Ziff, "The Ethical Dimension of 'The Custom-House,'" *Modern Language Notes* 73 (1958): 338–44; Sam S. Baskett, "*The* (Complete) *Scarlet Letter*," *College English* 22 (1961): 321–28; Frank MacShane, "The House of the Dead: Hawthorne's Custom House and *The Scarlet Letter*," *New England Quarterly* 35 (1962): 93–101; Marshall Van Deusen, "Narrative Tone in 'The Custom-House' and *The Scarlet Letter*," *Nineteenth-Century Fiction* 21 (1966): 61–71; David Stouck, "The Surveyor of 'The Custom-House': A Narrator for *The Scarlet Letter*," *The Centennial Review* 15 (1971): 309–29; James M. Cox, "The Scarlet Letter: Through The Old Manse and The Custom House," *Virginia Quarterly Review* 51 (1975): 432–47; and John Franzosa, " 'The Custom-House,' *The Scarlet Letter* and Hawthorne's Separation from Salem," *ESQ* 24 (1978): 57–71. For more general treatments of narrative unreliability in the novel, see Harry C. West, "Hawthorne's Editorial Pose," *American Literature* 44 (1972): 208–21; John G. Bayer, "Narrative Techniques and the Oral Tradition in *The Scarlet Letter*," *American Literature* 52 (1980): 250–63; and especially Elaine Tuttle Hansen, "Ambiguity and the Narrator in *The Scarlet Letter*," *The Journal of Narrative Technique* 5 (1975): 147–63. Although I disagree with Hansen's equation of ambiguity and moral openness, I have profited greatly from her sensitivity to narrative contradictions.

18 For "vanishings" in the preface, see pp. 22, 24. For Emerson's denial of books, see CW, vol. I, pp. 55–58; and for his famous use of "glad," see CW, vol. I, pp. 10, 288.

19 CW, vol. I, p. 53. There may be an especially close relationship between "The American Scholar" and "The Custom-House." Since the time of Holmes, Emerson's oration has been recognized as America's declaration of literary independence. Yet there is an implicit contradiction in Emerson's apparent jingoism and his Transcendental otherworldliness. As "The Custom-House" makes clear, literary independence is as much *from* America as *for* it. The narrator must finally renounce the Custom-House, politics, and America altogether to become a citizen of somewhere else, effectively a citizen of nowhere. For Aristophanes's creation myth, see Plato, *The Symposium*, 189a–193d. For more general references to the One Mind in Emerson, see CW, vol. II, pp. 3, 37–38, 160.

20 A similar denial is made in the prefatory letter to Bridge in *The Snow Image* (vol. XI, pp. 3–4). Hawthorne does occasionally speak about "real Mes," but only in the sentimental letters to his wife. See *Love*

Letters of Nathaniel Hawthorne, 1839–1863 (1907; reprint Washington, D.C.: NCR Microcard Editions, 1972), vol. I, pp. 225–6; vol. II, pp. 36, 78–79.

21 Emerson first makes this distinction, borrowed from Fichte and Carlyle, in *Nature* (CW, vol. I, p. 8). The distinction is so common in Emerson that Melville parodies it, in Chapter 7 of *Moby-Dick*, as one of the signs of Ishmael's naive Transcendentalism; see *Moby-Dick*, ed. Harrison Hayford and Hershel Parker (New York: Norton, 1967), p. 41.

22 Although in my account I tend to equate Hester with the male characters as equally misguided, I do not mean to comment one way or the other on the issue of Hawthorne's feminism. Hawthorne's admiration for Hester does not seem to me inconsistent with his criticism of her moral and intellectual position. Condescension, not criticism, is the true mark of chauvinist hostility; and Miss Birdseye, not Zenobia, is the way the male establishment revenges itself on the strong woman. The classic statement of the book's feminism is Leslie Fiedler, *Love and Death in the American Novel*, rev. ed. (New York: Dell, 1966), pp. 222–39; for a recent reading, see David Leverenz, "Mrs. Hawthorne's Headache: Reading *The Scarlet Letter*," *Nineteenth-Century Fiction* 37 (1983): 552–75.

23 The sumptuary habits of the Puritans are a recurring theme in the novel. See, for example, the discussion of Bellingham's ruff (pp. 108–9) and the Election Day procession (pp. 230–2). For a modern attack on the false notion of Puritan asceticism, see Perry Miller and Thomas M. Johnson, eds., *The Puritans* (New York: American Book Company, 1938), pp. 1–3.

24 The rare use of the term "mystic" in both passages to describe the letter may reinforce our sense that Hawthorne wants the reader to recognize the contradiction. For the only other such use of "mystic" in the novel, see p. 246.

25 I explore the other dimension of this scene – its relation to Hawthorne's theory of the romance – in my paper "Moonlight and Moonshine: The Irrelevance of Hawthorne's Prefaces," MLA, December 1983, which I hope soon to publish. Since the work of Richard Chase, commentary on this passage – and the four novel prefaces in general – has been enormous. For recent treatments, see Leo B. Levy, "The Notebook Source and 18th Century Context of Hawthorne's Theory of Romance," *Nathaniel Hawthorne Journal* 3 (1973): 120–9; Richard H. Brodhead, *Hawthorne, Melville, and the Novel* (Chicago: University of Chicago Press, 1976), pp. 29–42; Edgar A Dryden,

Nathaniel Hawthorne: The Poetics of Enchantment (Ithaca, N.Y.: Cornell University Press, 1977), pp. 120–42; and, for a more sociological approach, Michael Davitt Bell, *The Development of the American Romance: The Sacrifice of Relation* (Chicago: University of Chicago Press, 1980), pp. 127–55.

26 For language that similarly associates Hester (negatively) with twilight indistinctness, see pp. 84, 226. On the general ambiguity of light and color imagery in the novel, see Hyatt H. Waggoner, *Hawthorne, a Critical Study*, rev. ed. (Cambridge, Mass.: Harvard University Press, 1963), pp. 127–38.

27 Often Hawthorne presents a passage as if it were an omniscient description and then follows it with a phrase (like "thoughts like these") to indicate that in fact the language is the character's own. The unsettling effect is first to make the passage seem far more reliable than it is, and then by qualification to call attention to its unreliability (without quite erasing our original sense of its authoritativeness). For examples of this technique, see pp. 89–90, 206–7.

28 This dilemma has often been read as a mark of Hawthorne's own ambivalence, his emotional commitment to Hester's position in spite of his moral condemnation of her sin. For the classic early formulation of this position, see Frederic I. Carpenter, "Scarlet A Minus," *College English* 5 (1944): 173–80. For an attempt to reconcile this generally religious approach with a more cosmic, even mythic interpretation, see Roy R. Male, *Hawthorne's Tragic Vision* (New York: Norton, 1964), pp. 90–118. An even more general approach imagines the ambivalence to rest in Hawthorne's conflicting attractions to Puritanism and Transcendentalism. For the classic early formulation, see Randall Stewart, *American Literature and Christian Doctrine* (Baton Rouge: Louisiana State University Press, 1958), pp. 83–9. For a recent, highly sophisticated version, see John Carlos Rowe, "The Internal Conflict of Romantic Narrative: Hegel's Phenomenology and Hawthorne's *The Scarlet Letter*," *Modern Language Notes* 95 (1980): 1203–31.

29 P. 263. See also Dimmesdale's distinction between "penance" and "penitence," p. 192. A similar comparison between merely public "shame" and moral "guilt" runs throughout the novel. As with Dimmesdale's distinction, the implication is that Hester's shame is not true guilt and therefore signals no true repentance. See, for example, p. 80.

30 On the problem of symbolism and meaning in the novel, the seminal statements are those of Charles Feidelson, Jr., in his *Symbolism and American Literature* (Chicago: University of Chicago Press, 1953), pp. 6–12; and in "*The Scarlet Letter*," *Hawthorne Centenary Essays*, ed. Roy

Harvey Pearce (Columbus: Ohio State University Press, 1964), pp. 31–77. See also Millicent Bell, "The Obliquity of Signs," *Massachusetts Review* 23 (1982): 9–26.

31 See, for example, p. 57. The adjective "fair" seems similarly to mask sexist implications beneath more neutral indications of quantity or color. The "fair authority" for linking the rose bush to Ann Hutchinson identifies the legend as both reasonable and especially common among women (p. 48; cf. p. 50).

32 See especially the puns on "order" and "design," pp. 100–1.

33 See, for example, pp. 14, 26, 29, 78, 79, 144, 229, 230 (2), 236.

34 On the epistemological irrelevance of Brown's ambiguities, see David Levin, "Shadows of Doubt: Specter Evidence in Hawthorne's 'Young Goodman Brown,'" *American Literature* 34 (1962): 344–52; and Michael J. Colacurcio, "Visible Sanctity and Specter Evidence: The Moral World of Hawthorne's 'Young Goodman Brown,'" *Essex Institute Historical Collections* 110 (1974): 259–99.

35 For a good survey of the critical problems associated with Dimmesdale, see Darrel Abel, "Hawthorne's Dimmesdale: Fugitive from Wrath," *Nineteenth-Century Fiction* 11 (1956): 81–105. For a special focus on the ambiguities of his final scenes, see Thomas F. Walsh, Jr., "Dimesdale's Election Sermon," *Emerson Society Quarterly* 44 (1966): 64–6; and especially Terence Martin, "Dimmesdale's Ultimate Sermon," *Arizona Quarterly* 27 (1971): 230–40. The finest reading of the psychological dimensions of Dimmesdale's guilt is Frederick C. Crews, *The Sins of the Fathers: Hawthorne's Psychological Themes* (New York: Oxford University Press, 1966), pp. 136–53.

36 See also pp. 85, 246–7. It may be that the obviousness of some of the text's more traditional literary allusions – to Shakespeare and Milton, for example – is equally meant to call attention to the unreality of the fiction. See pp. 39, 79, 90.

37 The difference in the kinds of linguistic theories at work is evident in the sentence immediately following, where the narrator (perhaps in Hester's voice) redefines the burning shame as a real fire and Hester's bosom as the heart of her soul – her "breast" (the singular is significant).

38 Chillingworth's "dark necessity" recalls the extent to which similar language elsewhere in Hawthorne measures the characters' willingness to escape the moral and epistemological consequences of a situation by writing it of as incomprehensibly "dark." See especially Elizabeth's rejection of Hooper's veil and Rosina's of Roderick's snake as "dark fantasies" (vol. IX, p. 47; vol. X, p. 283).

39 Virtually all readers of the novel consider Pearl as purely symbolic, an aesthetic failure; in fact, one version of literary history treats Huck Finn as the realistic child who saved American literature from the twin excesses of Pearl and Little Eva. An interesting exception is Henry James, who seems to see in Pearl the prototype of his own representative but hardly allegorical heiresses. See his *Hawthorne* (1879; reprint London: Macmillan, 1967), especially pp. 108, 112, 115. For a good overview, see Barbara Garlitz, "Pearl: 1850–1955," *PMLA* 72 (1957): 689–99.

40 For the notebook sources, see vol. VIII, pp. 398–436, esp. pp. 420–1, 430–1. Where the observation is identical, the tone is different. In all cases, comparisons presented whimsically by Hawthorne are given far more weight in the novel by Hester and the narrator.

41 On the relation of Digby to Hawthorne, see Alfred S. Reid, "Hawthorne's Humanism: 'The Birthmark' and Sir Kenelm Digby," *American Literature* 38 (1966): 337–51. There is also a somewhat more predictable reference to the early scientist Paracelsus on p. 72 (cf. vol. X, p. 48). I have placed Digby (and Paracelsus) in a larger scientific context in my "Aylmer's Library: Transcendental Alchemy in Hawthorne's 'The Birthmark,'" *ESQ* 22 (1976): 211–20. For examples of the related terms "influence" and "impression," see pp. 36, 157, 239, 249, and pp. 164, 214, 216, 217, 259, respectively. In the case of both terms, the specific scientific (and all too palpable) meaning of the word undercuts any more general Romantic meaning and results in such slyly comic statements as those about the "impression" made on the crowd by Dimmesdale's letter (itself another kind of impression).

42 See "Homoeopathy and Its Kindred Delusions" in *The Works of Oliver Wendell Holmes*, Artists' Edition, vol. IX (Boston: Houghton, Mifflin, 1892), pp. 1–102. This lecture, delivered in Boston in 1842 and published shortly afterward, may well have been a source for Hawthorne's knowledge of the alchemical tradition. It is at least a good measure of what the educated nineteenth-century American can be expected to know about the pseudosciences. Digby is mentioned (pp. 8–10), as are birthmarks (pp. 27–8). More generally, Holmes focuses on homeopathy's theory that like cures like – a theory that originated in Paracelsian chemistry, and to which birthmark theory, with its assumption of the connection between mind and matter, might be considered a corollary. For an analysis of Hawthorne's conflation of Renaissance magic and contemporary science in "The Birth-mark," see H. Bruce

Franklin, *Future Perfect: American Science Fiction of the Nineteenth Century* (New York: Oxford University Press, 1966), pp. 9–16.

43 Huntington Library manuscript HM 10947. The published version of this letter – in *Love Letters*, vol. II, pp. 62–6 – is accurate except for two accidentals and the omission of a nasty comment about Sophia's sister Elizabeth.

44 For examples of symptom language, see pp. 136, 149, 155, 188. In the last, especially telling one, Hester unwittingly deflates Dimmesdale's Byronic agony by finding in him "no symptom of positive and vivacious suffering."

45 Sometimes "spiritual" is the term used for this realm halfway between soul and matter. The history of the "spiritus" or ether includes most of the major scientific minds of the modern world – not merely Ficino, Agrippa, Paracelsus, and Swedenborg, but Bacon, Descartes and Newton as well. For a general background, see D. P. Walker, *Spiritual and Demonic Magic from Ficino to Campanella* (London: Warburg Institute, 1958). For a useful summary of the ether and its relation to problems of materialism, see Cotton Mather's version of it, the *Nishmath-Chajim*, in *Angel*, pp. 28–38. It is this context that Mather first discusses birthmarks (p. 31). Poe discusses the ether as a failure of the imagination in *Eureka, Works*, vol. XVI, pp. 303–9.

46 For examples of "medium" in the novel, see pp. 35, 91, 123, 144, 176, 243, 263. For Emerson, see "Experience," CW, vol. III, p. 31; for Holmes, see *Works*, vol. IX, p. 2. Holmes's statement may allude explicitly to Swedenborg's famous claim that with a powerful enough microscope he could detect the soul; quoted in Signe Toksvig, *Emanuel Swedenborg, Scientist and Mystic* (New Haven, Conn.: Yale University Press, 1948), p. 87. For the classic Transcendentalist rejection of such pseudospiritualism, which they connected most closely with the eighteenth century and Hartley's associationism, see James Freeman Clarke's refusal to explain the soul in terms of vibrating nerve endings; quoted in Perry Miller, ed., *The Transcendentalists: An Anthology* (Cambridge, Mass.: Harvard University Press, 1950), pp. 47–8. Dugald Stewart delineates a similar tradition of the "materiality of ideas" and includes Digby in it; see his *Collected Works*, vol. V (Edinburgh: Thomas Constable & Co., 1854), pp. 137–48.

47 The notion of "spirit's nutriment" is altogether too literal. Yet such literalness is well within the historical tradition. Scientific texts and magic books alike recommend the consumption of "spiritual" foods – like gold – as a means of spiritualizing the body. See, for example, Walker, *Spiritual and Demonic Magic*, pp. 13–14; and Agrippa, *Occult*

Philosophy, pp. 522–3. See also Aylmer's love as an "aliment," vol. X, p. 36; Agrippa himself uses this term to describe spiritual food.

48 For "The Christmas Banquet," see vol. X, pp. 304–5. For Waldo's death, see CW, vol. III, p. 29.

49 James was the first to note (and object to) Hawthorne's obsession with the terms, used at least thirty-six times in the novel (see *Hawthorne*, p. 115). For the fullest treatment, see Roy R. Male, Jr., "Hawthorne and the Concept of Sympathy," *PMLA* 68 (1953): 138–49. See also Male, "Sympathy – a key word in American Romanticism," *Emerson Society Quarterly* 35 (1964): 19–23; and William R. Manierre, "The Role of Sympathy in *The Scarlet Letter*," *Texas Studies in Literature and Language* 13 (1971): 497–507. For uses of the term in the novel, see pp. 3, 9, 50, 64, 67, 69, 75, 86, 87, 89, 93, 113, 124, 138, 140, 142, 160, 161, 175, 179, 181, 184, 193, 200, 203, 205, 222, 226, 228, 231, 239, 243 (2), 246, 254, 256.

50 On the place of sympathy in eighteenth-century ethics and aesthetics, see M. H. Abrams, *The Mirror and the Lamp: Romantic Theory and the Critical Tradition* (New York: Oxford University Press, 1953), pp. 245, 247, 332; and James Engell, *The Creative Imagination: Enlightenment to Romanticism* (Cambridge, Mass.: Harvard University Press, 1981), pp. 143–60; and for the American tradition, Norman Fiering, *Jonathan Edwards's Moral Thought and Its British Context* (Chapel Hill: University of North Carolina Press for the Institute of Early American History and Culture, Williamsburg, Va., 1981), pp. 138–44.

51 "Of the Sympathetick Powder: A Discourse in a Solemn Assembly at Montepellier" (London: John Williams, 1669), p. 180; usually bound with Digby's *Two Treatises* (1669). It is in this work that Digby discusses birthmarks (pp. 179–89). Holmes summarizes the experiment, although not the explanation in *Works*, vol. IX, pp. 8–10.

52 On Roderick's pride, see vol. X, p. 274. Goodman Brown's despair may be a kind of inverted pride; see vol. X, pp. 88–90. Although Mr. Hooper seems more generous in his evaluation of his own superiority to others, some critics read a secret pride in his smile; see vol. IX, pp. 41, 52. Gervayse Hastings' similar smile surely marks his proud sense of his right to attend the ghastly banquets; see vol. X, pp. 290, 292.

53 See especially CW, vol. I, pp. 15–16. It is at least this chapter of *Nature* to which Hawthorne alludes explicitly in "The Old Manse," vol. X, p. 5; cf. vol. I, p. 13.

54 Not only is moonlight a "medium" and firelight an "influence." The whole description speaks the language of Renaissance mechanics: "This warmer light [of coal] mingles itself with the cold spirituality of

the moonbeams, and communicates, as it were, a heart and sensibilities of human tenderness to the forms which fancy summons up" (p. 36). And in fact, Digby's treatise on the powder of sympathy does contain a strikingly similar description of how to wash one's hands with moonlight (pp. 162–[163], misprinted "193").

55 In one sense, the fundamental theory on which visible sanctity, birthmarks, and hypocrisy all depend is the correspondence theory of truth – the notion that truth consists in the coincidence between belief and fact. The alternative coherence theory studies the way in which beliefs hang together in a system – whether defined elaborately, as in German idealism, or loosely, as in modern Wittgensteinian and pragmatic accounts. My reading in general discovers in Hawthorne's emphasis on the materialist implications of correspondence an implicit argument for pragmatic semantics in *The Scarlet Letter*.

56 For representative uses of the term, see pp. 127, 140, 190, 207, 255 (2), and, of course, the title to the penultimate chapter.

57 The famous sentence – "The scarlet letter had not done its office" (p. 166) – may operate on two levels. Most simply, Hawthorne and the narrator agree that the letter has failed in both of its common functions: to chasten Hester by reminding her of her error and to warn others of the seriousness of that act. The narrator, however, may imply more in his choice of the portentous word "office." If the word is meant to carry religious overtones – to turn Hester's punishment into a kind of improvised sacrament – then the statement, by overinvesting in the power of meaning, does not so much describe the failure as reenact it. On this point, of course, Hawthorne would not agree with his narrative persona.

58 James makes this objection on p. 106.

59 In the novel, the language of inmosts and lives within life is usually questioned, most often in the context of Dimmesdale's hyperactive self-scrutiny. See, for example, pp. 74, 80, 140, 143, 146, 217, 255. For similar reservations elsewhere in Hawthorne, see especially "Egotism" (vol. X, p. 274) and "The Christmas Banquet" (vol. X, p. 301). For an example of Emerson's use of the notion of a life within life, in a section appropriately entitled "Reality," see "Experience" (CW, vol. III, pp. 41–2).

60 Surely this is the conclusion that Emerson himself reached. In the passage from "Experience" quoted earlier, idealism – redefined as subjectiveness – becomes the "Fall of Man," an epistemological indeterminacy to which all things, including God, merely tumble in (CW, vol. III, pp. 43–4).

61 The real goal of epistemology is not so much certainty as a delimitation of the knowable to define by contrast what cannot be known but only believed: in Kant's formulation, the denial of knowledge to make room for faith; or, in Wittgenstein's, the wisdom to pass over in silence that about which we cannot speak.

"The Woman's Own Choice": Sex, Metaphor, and the Puritan "Sources" of *The Scarlet Letter*

MICHAEL J. COLACURCIO

1

THE problem with "source criticism" is that it raises more questions than it answers. Or else, as often as not, it discovers questions where none before existed. We always wish to read the works our author has read; yet we quickly discover that a text is easier to read "in itself," as we used to say, than as a function of what we now call its "pretexts." Further, the discovery that some apparently unified and powerfully original work of literary imagination actually reveals traces of other works usually leaves us a little let down: Evidently the myth of uninfluenced identity, defeated in life, had wished to live on in literary criticism. And finally, the presence of those traces instantly generates a whole new set of difficulties, at a level quite different from the one on which they were first discovered. Why this particular pretext and not others? (Don't *all* roads lead to Xanadu?) Is the trace in question an unconscious echo or a deliberate allusion? If unconscious, is it therefore accidental and meaningless? If deliberate, is it yet the sort of necessary "borrowing" an author has tried but failed to conceal? Or is it in fact part of a pattern or purpose, a constitutive element in some strategic design of repetition and difference?

In this last case most of all — but in the others too, in some fair degree — we always want to know what *else* the positive identification of a source can possibly teach us. And this added fact is not always easy to learn. Hawthorne's texts rewrite those of the Puritans. Yet what critical significance are we supposed to attach to that information? Was Hawthorne himself therefore a Puritan? Or just a little short on plots? Or else somehow anxious to disguise present psychic interest as past religious theme?

But to remain with the general case just a moment longer: Evidently our discomfort is most acute when a source or pretext turns out to be "historical," rather than "literary," in the ordinary (but now embattled) sense of that word. Books that allude to Shakespeare or Milton may betray, thereby, their want of absolute originality, but clearly they have nothing to fear by way of generic reduction. The texts speak to *one another,* we tend to assume, and at a level of privilege so rare that no real violation can occur; thus, we spread out an *order* of literature that retains its purity, even if no individual literary text is ever completely "originary." But what if the pretext is not Milton but Cotton Mather, not Shakespeare but John Winthrop? Suddenly the noble kingdom comes under attack. Wordsworth's response to Milton founds the modernist project. But what supposable canon can ever be constituted by folding Winthrop's *History of New England* into *The Scarlet Letter*? Only that of "American Studies," presumably, where literary appreciation usually takes a back seat to intellectual or social history?

And yet the evidence accumulates. If the geography and physical setting of *The Scarlet Letter* reveal an author who wrote with Caleb Snow's *History of Boston* "on the desk,"[1] the moral setting and even, in some deep sense, the plot evidently required of Hawthorne – and may yet demand of us – a pretty fair recall of the matters John Winthrop set out as the essential religious and political story of the first two decades of his holy experiment and Model City. The matter of Ann Hutchinson we may now take for granted. Although elaborated by Winthrop in a separate book on the very subject, and then significantly reviewed in Cotton Mather's comprehensive *Magnalia,* the Hutchinson story exists most essentially in the *Journal,* where it figures as something like the definitive (if negative) test case of Winthrop's own special theory of covenant as a fusion of law and love; and it is from that source, primarily, that Hawthorne was moved to create, in Hester Prynne, a female protagonist whose primary distinction is to walk "in the footsteps" of Ann Hutchinson.[2]

A complicated story, to be sure, but even simpler evidence has pointed in the same direction. The classic source study of *The Scarlet Letter* had wanted to emphasize externals out of Snow's *History,* but it was unable to suppress the implication that both the career and *Journal* of John Winthrop moved everywhere, just beneath the surface. A well nigh definitive essay on the problem of "Public Confession" and *The Scarlet Letter* returns again and again to that crucial document for its most suggestive hints and analogs. And a most able treatment of Hawthorne's connections with the conventions of "Historical Romance" must strenuously insist that Winthrop ("the founding father *par excellence*") well survives his intriguing displacement by the altogether unliterary figure of Richard Bellingham.[3] So that the time may well have come to test, however tentatively, a very suggestive proposition about the intertextual status of Hawthorne's most powerful evocation of the Puritan world — namely, that Winthrop's famous *Journal* is not only a prime and obvious source for Hawthorne's knowledge of "historical backgrounds" but that it furnishes the novel's most essential themes; that Winthrop's record may itself be a vital part of Hawthorne's own (intensely historical) subject.[4]

A full exposition of that complex proposition would require, eventually, a monograph three or four times the space allotted here. It would involve, among other things, a full (and fully literary) reading of the structure and theme of Winthrop's *Journal* itself — and that in relation to the work of many other Puritan writers who struggle to harmonize the matters of law and love. It would require an elaboration of the entire seriousness of historical fiction, in a literary climate where such a thing has seemed either "popular" or Marxist. And it would demand some account of why Hawthorne might have felt intellectually compelled (rather than personally obsessed) by Winthrop's own peculiar mix of moral and political matter. But one has to begin somewhere. And, as Hawthorne himself everywhere implies, there's no time like the past.

2

Clearly, the narrator of *The Scarlet Letter* — however criticism shall come to identify his exact relation to Hawthorne himeslf — knows a great deal more about the Puritan world of the 1630s and 1640s than he will forcefully obtrude on the notice of the less knowledgeable readers he alternatively assures and provokes. And much of his learning appears to come, ultimately at least, from Winthrop's *Journal,* which *no* historian of the Massachusetts "Utopia" (p. 47)[5] can escape rewriting, in one way or another. As Bradford's *Plymouth* is someplace else, only Winthrop was present at *this* creation, of which his own prefatory "Model of Christian Charity" served as moral groundplan and exemplar. Yet our narrator also knows enough not to trust either our native sense of plausibility or our knowledge of actual events. And so, before his own narrative has had the time it usually takes an extended fiction to develop a life entirely its own, he challenges us with an anxious-making reminder that his story really does presuppose a prefictive, "historical" world. About which it will help us to know.

The clearest example is unmistakable indeed. No sooner, fictionally speaking, has Hester settled down to "Her Needle" (Chapter 5), and to the "morbid purpose" (p. 90) of outfitting "Pearl" (Chapter 6) as her own scarlet letter in human form, than she finds herself called upon to justify the quality and effect of her Christian nurture.[6] Of course, the logic of her inquisitors is perfectly pernicious and circular, a theological "Catch 22" hardly designed to increase our regard for the "New England mind": If Pearl were "of demon origin," then "a Christian interest in the mother's soul required" the guardians of the Covenant to "remove such a stumbling-block from her path." Or – dichotomy as undistributed middle – if the child were indeed human, "then, surely, it would enjoy all the fairer prospect [of salvation] by being transferred to wiser and better guardianship" (p. 100). The modern reader may wonder how any of this "logic" comports with the decree of predestination; perhaps Hawthorne's Puritans are no more simply Calvinist than those of Perry Miller. But the narrator has other, simpler worries: Won't the reader think his psychological romance is taking absurd plot liberties with the political realities of history, thereby slandering the past? And so, in a rather remarkable moment of direct address, he elaborately cautions that reader to remember exactly what sort of a world he has entered.

His sober little disclaimer is worth quoting in its entirety:

> It may appear singular, and indeed not a little ludicrous, that an affair of this kind, which, in later days, would have been referred to no higher jurisdiction than that of the selectmen of the town,

should then have been a question publicly discussed, and on which statesmen of eminence took sides. At that epoch of pristine simplicity, however, matters of even slighter public interest, and of far less intrinsic weight, than the welfare of Hester and her child, were strangely mixed up with the deliberations of legislators and acts of state. The period was hardly, if at all, earlier than that of our story, when a dispute concerning the right of property in a pig not only caused a fierce and bitter contest in the legislative body of the colony, but resulted in an important modification of the framework itself of the legislature. (p. 101)

Clearly there are enough ironies here to keep us busy for a long time. And again, our first response may involve simple and extreme dismay: Trying to justify what, from a later perspective, can only seem an unwarrantable intrusion of federal power into an entirely local (or congregational) matter — if not a positive invasion of privacy — our narrator actually succeeds in trivializing the entire process and product of constitutional development in Massachusetts. Surely modern readers merely smile when, elsewhere, a cautious and worldly man like John Winthrop suggests that something of the mind of God may be discovered by studying which parts of a religious book will and will not be consumed by mice. And perhaps we can yet believe it a "majestic idea, that the destiny of nations should be revealed, in [the] awful hieroglyphics, on the cope of heaven" (p. 155). But what order of history or Providence can we possibly invoke when our own system of separation of powers turns out to have been invented by a pig?[7] Especially when the same animal fable tells so unhappily against the status of Hester's precious child.

Perhaps the narrator has intended his vicious reductionism: Hester on the scaffold has already seemed a Pearl cast before swine; and evidently he thinks that figure may obtain wherever the mysteries of the human soul are forcefully opened to the view of a disciplinary, punishing public. But somewhere the irony is supposed to go deeper, as it surely will for any reader willing to be guided back to the necessary pretext of this nowise innocent little history lesson.

Practitioners of American Studies will know the story of the Pig that Divided the Legislature from the pages of Samuel Eliot Morison's masterful (if somewhat filiopietistic) *Builders of the Bay Colo-*

105

ny: The typically American form of bicameral legislature came into view just when, in the case of the disputed ownership of a pig, the Magistrates successfully reversed the judgment of the Deputies, thus making good at last their long-standing claim to enjoy the power of veto (or "negative voice"), and pointing the way, thereby, to some future sense of upper and lower houses, without benefit of any Federalist fantasy of an American peerage. In itself a ridiculous instance, of course, but the Lord moves in strange ways, and when was typology *ever* a respecter of persons? Much the same lesson may be drawn, fairly enough, from the version Hawthorne himself had (unquestionably) read in Snow's *History of Boston*, which "source critics" may always insist is the real inspiration for Hawthorne's curious aside.[8] But the serious reader of historical fiction may well feel himself invited to pursue the tale back to its ultimate source, from which Snow's nineteenth-century account is itself obviously derivative: the firsthand, eyewitness, participant's account in Winthrop's *Journal*, without which the story would not have survived at all.

The specific reference would be to an entry for June 22, 1642 – a date that, on other grounds, we might wish to fix as the absolute beginning of *The Scarlet Letter*'s own scaffold-scene action.[9] But the episode is crucial to a story and a logic that extend both backward and forward from this specific moment; and that, along with the story and logic of the "rise, reign, and ruin" of those libertine familists we know as the antinomians, make Winthrop's *Journal* an organized and vital history rather than a series of needful annals. Taking close account of the sexual crimes eventually perpetrated by all those who espoused the higher liberty of the Spirit, Winthrop is equally watchful of all arguments for civil privileges greater than those granted by the Massachusetts charter or logically consistent with his own sense of the nature of human government. Indeed, the "theme" of the *Journal* is precisely those excesses committed in the name of some liberty, of nature or of their charter, other than that implied in his initial definition of "charity," according to which civil order is altogether impossible without a number of severe (and recognizable) forms of subordination. And although Winthrop is glad of the political triumph of his upper house of fully chartered Magistrates, his more somber concern, here as elsewhere, is for the whole tenor of political wrangling about "rights" that give it context. The mordant realism of his earlier comment remains in force: "how strictly the people would seem to stick to their patent, where they think it makes for their advantage."[10]

What emerges from the restrained and largely unrhetorical pages of Winthrop's *Journal,* from the beginning, and down to the mid-1640s at least, is the sad and often exasperated feeling that a whole variety of misunderstandings about liberty are abroad in his land. On the one hand, obviously, but not quite originally, a few antinomians – "bold sensualists," as Emerson might have called them – were invoking spiritual liberty to cover their own sexual license; on the other, a rising and all too politicized populace was demanding ever greater legal clarification and political voice. Apparently, almost everyone wanted a full and written set of "positive laws," to specify Moses and to limit the discretionary authority of the godly Magistrates. Worse yet, a party of Freemen were quibbling and quarreling in ways that forced a single, precarious territorial guarantee to bear the undue strain of full constitutional development. Lust, Wintrhop must have felt, he would always have with him. But hermeneutics he had hoped to avoid.

What is signaled by the narrator's curious aside, then, in Winthrop's American Ur-world and in his own most orderly imitation, is the presence of an extreme political anxiety at the heart of the Puritan system, uncertainty and strife where there should have been sweet consensus. Pious wish had fathered no stable political fact. A world where a pig can alter a legislature is a world of flux, in which any novel decision might yet produce the most unlooked-for and far-reaching consequences. And the reader who feared monolithic unity was just plain wrong.

Suddenly the *dis*agreements hinted at in the chapters of Hester's exposure and judgment come into sharp thematic prominence. The narrator's explicit sense of violent moral "outrage" (p. 55) is set against his subtler evocation of political confusion and even experimentation. Sensing legal ambiguity as well as moral complexity, perhaps, the "magistracy . . . have not been bold to put in force the extremity of our righteous law against her" (p. 63), which is, as a particularly ugly member of the female populace has

107

already reminded us, death, "both in the Scripture and the statute-book" (pp. 51–2). Suddenly, Hester seems caught up in the midst of a constitutional crisis, at a moment of historical unfolding that is arguably more "crucial" than of the "Antinomian Controversy" of the 1630s.[11] An entire "way" is at issue. And, unless Hawthorne himself is being both prurient and reductive, the whole crisis seems to take Hester's "adultery" as its fitting symbol. Superficially, at least, Winthrop had tried to keep his sexual cases separate from his political ones. But here they stand wholly conflated, leaving readers to wonder what strange principal of fictional displacement can substitute Hester herself (rather than Pearl) for Winthrop's problematic pig.

The answer is complicated, as we may fairly expect. And it requires that we stay *with* the Winthrop source – literally, still, and well before we should think to tease out its own sexual politics. But the invitation (possibly a demand) is clearly present in Hawthorne's text. And this time, it points to its own most outrageous manipulation of history: the problem of "Governor" Bellingham.

The same chapter that seeks to defend Hester's summons to "The Governor's Hall" (Chapter 7) actually begins with a political reminder of a lower order, but one that turns out to involve us in *The Scarlet Letter*'s famous historical "mistake." Remember, it says, that by "now" (1645) the man we're calling "Governor Bellingham" is no longer the actual governor of Massachusetts. Yet the course of fact or probability is scarcely violated, "for, though the changes of a popular election had caused this former ruler to descend a step or two from the highest rank, he still held an honorable and influential place among the colonial magistracy" (p. 100). Once again, but with results even more devastating, the narrative evokes ironies that survive and all but swamp the factual disclaimer. Specifically, we are being reminded that, even as a *mere* magistrate, Bellingham commands considerable judicial authority, although obviously much less than he had that day in June 1642 when he stood on the balcony of judgment above Hester's scaffold of shame. And yet, it is this very reminder – of the political ouster of Bellingham – that forces us to advert to the lie we had originally been led to believe: The real-life governor of Massachusetts Bay in

108

June 1642 had been John Winthrop; Bellingham's political defeat had occurred the month before. For reasons we need to think seriously about, the narrative is now fussing about niceties where before it had flatly said the thing which was not.

In one sense, the news is not so new. Source critics have long known about the "displacement" of Winthrop by Bellingham; nor has responsible speculation failed to produce plausible explanations of why, within the conventions of Hawthorne's peculiar sub-genre, the sly little metonym seems justifiable and even necessary.[12] Yet looked at in the light of the information furnished by Winthrop's *Journal*, the matter seems the very reverse of innocent. Much more is at issue, evidently, than either the freedom or the mimetic exigencies of "romance." And, judged in that same light, the narrator's remark about "the chances of a popular election" turns out to be one of the most vicious lines Hawthorne ever penned.

Bellingham's political story, leading up to his defeat in the Great and General Election of May 1642, is, for one thing, about as unlike Hawthorne's own recent, more debatable dismissal from the Salem Custom-House as we could imagine.[13] Bellingham was, after all, himself the candidate rather than some mere pork-barrel appointee, and his own recent behavior formed the well-known substance of the political argument against him. Furthermore, that behavior had been explicitly sexual. Indeed it seems essentially accurate to say that Bellingham had been voted out of office, in May 1642, for conduct not so different from Hester's own. For which he was punished – somewhat unequally, as it may appear – with the sort of political reprimand that forced him "to descend a step or two from the highest rank." Evidently the *real* politics behind *The Scarlet Letter* are, quite apart from the ultimate implications of Winthrop's rhetoric, themselves intensely sexual.

Bellingham's story is not nice, but it is fairly simple. Widowed, at age fifty, and wishing to remarry, during the term of his own governorship, a young woman of twenty, he simply declared the wish a fact, on the strength of his own authority. No problem, as he may have thought: Puritan marriage being a civil affair, no benefit of clergy need apply; and was he not himself, at the time, the highest civil officer in the land? Yet Winthrop and many others were deeply distressed. Anxious to get on to other matters (including the case of the eighty-year-old Reverend Mr. Batchellor who, "having a lusty comely woman to his wife, [did] nevertheless solicit the chastity of his neighbor's wife"), Winthrop turns aside to point out that "the young gentlewoman was ready to be contracted to a friend of his, who lodged in his house." Then, conceding this point of honor, which Bellingham "excused . . . by the strength of his affection," he presses two more official charges: that Bellingham "would not have his contract published . . . contrary to an order of court," and that "he married himself, contrary to the constant practice of the country."[14] A strange covenant, this: no banns and no civil witness. Perhaps Bellingham felt that what he did "had a consecration of its own." Perhaps he and his stolen bride even "said so to each other" (p. 195).

The attempts at prosecution that followed proved ineffectual, as Bellingham refused to "go off the bench" for his own trial. But as Winthrop's later editor remarks, "After such an experience of Bellingham, it is not strange that the colony should restore its chief dignity to Winthrop once more in May, 1642."[15] And the reader of *The Scarlet Letter* is now in a position to grasp the wicked logic of its major historical fabrication. Bellingham and not Winthrop sentences Hester, for the keen historical irony involved: But for the grace of his magistracy (or his maleness?), there go he. Or, to put the matter less allusively, the demoted "Governor" Bellingham stood, in June 1642, not as the accuser but as the accused, in a rather tensely central case of sex and constitutionality in the unfolding experiment of utopian Massachusetts. A largely forgotten case, perhaps, except as *The Scarlet Letter* goes well out of its own fictional way to remind us.

At one level the joke is fairly nasty – rather like the local justice of the peace who, accustomed to rail against the morals of the young, is himself, one Saturday night, taken in adultery. Let him who is without sin . . . Yet here too the irony may go deeper. Possibly we are to wonder about the fate of the distinctive covenant of marriage in the midst of a society that is, on one side, redundantly overcovenanted already and, on the other, likely to produce prophetic critiques of all merely contractual arrangements. Winthrop believes in love, although he might begin by

110

calling it "charity." And he resolutely believes in the law, if only in the form of "an order of court." Yet how are these conflicting loyalties to be harmonized? How "like," in the end, are law and love?

At the very least, the "matter of Bellingham" reminds us just how literally sexual are the historical matters that lie at the "source" of *The Scarlet Letter*. Perhaps Hawthorne's romance is indeed more about sex than that "guilt" we used to notice, in dutiful recognition that the drama of the book itself is all painfully (if not quite penitentially) after the fact of Hester's unique act of intercourse. And if so, perhaps it is about that curious, slandered, but intensely historical subject of sex in the world of the Puritans. Not in the world of the "bourgeoisie," where texts enough already inspire the researches of Peter Gay or (at a more "powerful" level of discourse) Michel Foucault, but in the American seventeenth century.[16] The subject might be *only* — as we might say, fidgeting — metaphorical, since Hester does seem designed to "figure" something or other; and since, in the end, language (and its silences) *will* always come in the way. But perhaps even that possibility deserves further attention. Granting, for the moment, that all sex is the same elemental fact of nature — or even, more tendentiously, that the matter or theme of the triangle really is eternal — we may yet wish to ask if there was not perhaps something distinctive and revealing in the way Winthrop and his utopian Puritans thought and spoke about such matters. Certainly this is the implication of Bellingham's *other* sex scandal of 1641–2, which may also have left its traces in Hawthorne's text.

This second, really ugly case implicated Bellingham not as a principal but as a judge — and also, it oddly appears, as something of what we would now call a "sexologist." And it involved all of Puritan New England in a question we might associate with one of the more explicitly sexual utopias of the nineteenth century more readily than with Winthrop's (or Bellingham's) Boston — with Finney's Oberlin, for example, or with the Oneida Community of John Humphrey Noyes. Yet it truly appears that the anxiously developing legal establishment of Massachusetts (and Plymouth, Connecticut, and New Haven as well) needed to determine, just then and there, the true import of human sexuality: time out, so to

111

speak, while the facts of life are driven into a corner, assessed, and published to all those validly concerned. Specifically, the matter involved the question of "natural" and "unnatural" sexuality, including the prescribed scriptural penalties for sins of both sorts. But the *essential* question, or the "meaning" of sex itself, clearly lurked. And the reader of *The Scarlet Letter* needs to know that Hawthorne has ascribed the opening of his most explicitly sexual romance to the one moment when much of colonial New England seemed to have sex on its official and conscious mind.[17]

Although the (expurgated) twentieth-century version of Winthrop's *Journal* decently averts its gaze, the 1825–6 edition we know Hawthorne read gives all the lurid (or pathetic) details. The two prepubescent daughters of a certain John Humfry were re-peatedly "abused" – "especially on the Lord's days and lecture days" – by a series of "rude servants," and also by others of the better sort who happened to be, temporarily at least, men without women. These "very foul sin[s]" went for a long time unreported; yet they did eventually reach the light of Puritan mind.[18] As the matter became public, it fell to the court of the woman-snatching Bellingham to decide the appropriate penalty for what our own sociological wisdom calls sexual abuse of children. And because the question arose at the very moment when the nexus of *all* crime and punishment was publicly at issue, it drew forth the full sub-tlety of the Puritans' "scholastic" intellect, even as it paralyzed their legal machinery for the better part of two gubernatorial terms.

On the one hand (Jesus and the Pharisees to one side), the "judicials" of Moses clearly made adultery a capital crime, pre-cisely as Hawthorne's litigious matrons had been quick to observe; so that the *married* abusers could always be executed on that score. Yet something else seemed involved as well. Did not the age of the abused females essentially matter, even if one or the other seemed from time to time to consent and "[take] pleasure in it"? An earlier case had already aroused Winthrop's keenest legal faculty. A boy convicted of raping a child of 7 or 8 years old "escaped with a severe whipping" (the punishment for "single fornication") be-cause the penalty for rape "was not death by the law of God." And yet Winthrop suspected that "by equity of the law against sodomy, it should be death for a man to have carnal copulation with a girl so young, as there can be no possibility of generation, for it is against nature as well as sodomy and buggery."[19] And so in the present instance as well: Because the females in question were well below the age of childbearing, had not their *penetratio* (the records lapse into Latin) been significantly unnatural? Evidently the breach of sexual covenant was not the only source of capital matter.

Rational men may disagree, of course; and yet they needed to know the answer to the "great question" of "what kind of sin this was, whether sodomy, or rape, or etc." And so it fell to Bellingham, himself not *much* better than he should have been, to compose a sort of sexual questionnaire, seeking "to know the mind of God by the help of all the Elders of the country, both our own, and Plymouth, and Connecticut, New Haven, etc."[20] What he had to ask, of every duly constituted congregational officer, was what exactly rational men might understand the Pentateuch to mean by "sodomy"; and, more specifically, what precise acts of sexuality a Bible state was bound to regard as capital offenses.

The answers Bellingham received (a sample of which the modern reader may consult in the definitive edition of Bradford's *Plymouth*) are revealing in the extreme.[21] And more than a little depressing, perhaps, to anyone seriously anticipating "some brighter period" when a "new truth" should "establish the whole relation between men and women on a surer ground of mutual happiness" (p. 263). An *old* morality still, and with a vengeance.

Yet the point is not so much the number of sexual practices declared to be capitally sinful: Nothing significant is added by the observation that the world has since discovered it can tolerate a good deal more dysfunction, experiment, and preference than the Mosaic law supposed. Somewhat closer to the mark would be the observation of how little attention – namely, none – is given to the plight of the young females in question. Unmentioned except as the legal premise or sinful occasion, they are effectively reduced to animal status: Lying with them has been, evidently, a lot like lying with a ewe or a mare. And worst of all, perhaps, is the old-time ease with which the obscure teachings of Deuteronomy and Leviticus are referred back to some lucid and cleanly standard called "nature," leaving the reader to wonder how to name the urge whose expression had caused the case to arise in the first place. For surely we are reminded that, like so much else, the puritanic understanding of sexuality tended too readily to presume its competence to settle any contested point.

Everywhere the discussion centers on the question of *penetratio* versus *contactus et frictatio,* and everywhere the distinction between the natural and the unnatural is referred to some terribly material concept of "cleanness" – until one almost wonders if the two young women in question may be thought to have "chewed the cud and divided the hoof."[22] Thus, whatever sociopolitical logic operated to forgive the sexual of misdemeanor of Bellingham himself, the more primary categories that emerge from his questionnaire must be judged primitive indeed. Without at all applauding his own understanding of human sexuality, the reader of *The Scarlet Letter* is forced to conclude that the men who judge Hester Prynne do not appear to know what they are talking about; and that the famous displacement of Winthrop by Bellingham means to call attention to this unhappy fact.

Surely some such charge is implied by the arresting and otherwise highly gratuitous accusation made by the narrator as he seeks to characterize those judges. Granting that their somewhat spurious "dignity of mien" owes much "to a period when the forms of authority were felt to possess the sacredness of divine institutions," and conceding (with some irony, given what we know of Bellingham) that "they were doubtless, good men, just, and sage," he means nevertheless to impugn their present competence absolutely:

> Out of the whole human family, it would not have been easy to select the same number of wise and virtuous persons, who should be less capable of sitting in judgment on an erring woman's heart, and disentangling its mesh of good and evil, than the sages of rigid aspect towards whom Hester Prynne now turned her face. (p. 64)

A remarkable passage indeed, the reader is bound to feel, especially in a fiction that ends by praising Hester's return to serve the standards of the community so viciously attacked. Yet the present thought insists on itself: The men on the balcony above Hester are utterly unfit to "meddle with a question of human guilt, passion, and anguish" (p. 65). Whatever the biblical premises of their utopian state, their sexual categories are utterly inappropriate to the present instance.

And the relevance of the second Bellingham episode is only heightened when we learn the other questions in his timely little survey. A second seems to have asked for help in deciding – as in the legal inquisition surrounding the shame of Hester's sexual reduction – "how far a magistrate might exact a confession from a delinquent in capital cases." And then, filling out our sense of the historical mind in question, what is to be done "for the maintenance of the trade of beaver?"[23] So much for the "strangely mixed . . . deliberations" of that "epoch of pristine simplicity." And small wonder if the narrator should wish, illogically, for a "Papist among the crowd of Puritans": not that his canon law would seem, by comparison, a triumph of humane sensibility, prosing as it does about "the natural female vessel," but probably some remembered image of the "Divine Maternity" (p. 56) might fairly redress the uneven contextual balance. And surely that image would redeem Hester no more unfairly than she is degraded by the one more nearly provided – of an "iron-visaged" old dame replacing Hester's curiously stitched letter with "a rag of my own rheumatic [i.e., menstruous] flannel" (p. 54). Evidently it is very hard, the early scenes of *The Scarlet Letter* suggest, to take the right tone about sex. And no easier then, certainly, than now.

Yet those same scenes appear to suggest that this unsolvable problem is also a vital one, that Hester's sexual transgression stands at the center of and indeed epitomizes a highly public and utterly crucial moment in the development of the Puritans' model city. To be sure, the narrative will presently turn inward, to an exploration of Hester's own mixture of shame, hysteria, and even antinomian rebellion; and then, even more so, in the case of Dimmesdale, so that "The Interior of a Heart" (Chapter 11) can all too easily come to stand for the true domain of Hawthorne's "psychological romance." But at the outset, insistently, and throughout the rest of the tale, by intermittent reminders, we are forced to notice that Hester's deepest difficulty is that she has created a problem her peculiar world does not know how to address, let alone solve. And yet it is one that world feels it *must* solve if it is to

maintain its covenanted identity and get on with the task of elaborating its own peculiar institutions. Failure here is failure *simply,*
we are plainly led to feel. No ambiguities, please: "cemetery" and
"prison" in all realism provided (p. 47), let's get this awkward
affair of the flesh rationalized before the law and press on into the
Kingdom. What further need of witnesses, really? Mark her with
something and then get this City moving again.

Nor should most of this have ever been anything but obvious:
Hester challenges a whole community in an absolutely fundamental way, and the range of inappropriate attitudes taken by the
ministers, magistrates, and populace alike reveal the anxiety appropriate to the discovery that some splendid intellectual edifice
has been reared on a foundation of murk. Bellingham's questionnaire may betray no qualm appropriate to his own personal situation; possibly he thought of his own sin as altogether "natural."
Yet Winthrop's *Journal* eventually reveals the same sort of hesita-
tions that undid the splendid confidence of Bradford's *Plymouth* –
as antinomians, servants, even Christian magistrates all fall back
into the common, if multifarious, condition of natural desire.[24]
And so, ironically, it requires the meretricious rhetoric of the explicitly hypocritical Dimmesdale to lend the situation of Hester its
needful complexity; for evidently some "quality of awful sacredness" (p. 114) will always escape the utopian rationalism of the
judges she has to face. Even as they try to name all things to the
use of their own holy politics.

4

Yet the subtler implications of Hawthorne's studied historicism
evade us still. Granting that Bellingham's (fictional) judgments of
Hester are themselves significantly hypocritical, and that (historically) his sexual questionnaire epitomizes a *very* old morality; yet
no accomplished reader of Puritan literature can tolerate the slan-
derous implication that the builders of the Bay Colony were, to a
man, nothing but bourgeois legalists flourishing some quaint utopian metahistory. Winthrop, for example, was a fairly accomplished writer of love letters, and no one need accuse him of being
an "old man" who had "lived so long and forgotten so much that

[he could not] remember anything [he] ever knew or felt or even heard about love."[25] And other evidence indicates that the American Puritans did indeed possess their own highly developed idiom of the sexual sacred.

Of the first generation, only Cotton fully explicated the sacred love poetry of Canticles – and not so well, it may yet appear, as Edward Taylor later. Clearly, Cotton's rhetoric nowhere courts the transport of mystic sexuality. And the critic may even conclude that his American performances *plainly* eschew not only the pentecostal "Tongue of Flame" (p. 142) but even the more modest Dimmesdalean "eloquence and religious fervor" (p. 66). Still, his meditations on the "kisses of his mouth," which are "better than wine," are part of the relevant historical context; and evidently they matter in a tale that implicates Cotton almost as directly as Hutchinson.[26] And everywhere else, the reader of *The Scarlet Letter* needs to learn, the expounders of official Puritanism appropriated the facts of sexuality to the new life of grace and the church. "Weaned affections" was a lively cliché of Puritan poetry and preaching, not at all a dead metaphor: If one could give up sucking at the teat of the world, he would yet find sufficient nourishment "out of the Breasts of both Testaments."[27] So that the ironic career of "Governor" Richard Bellingham tells us only part of what we need to know about the sources of *The Scarlet Letter*'s sexual theme.

The now familiar story of Hester Prynne as a sort of literalized Ann Hutchinson tells us just a bit more: Hester's sexual threat to her holy community seems but Hawthorne's ironic embodiment of what Puritan rhetoric implied was really or deeply true of her historical counterpart. When Hutchinson taught spiritual liberty, including a liberation from the Pauline anxiety of mind and members, the Puritans could hear only a distinctively womanly licensing of the passional self; thus, a high Protestant heretic was reduced to a libertine, and to a wily (female) seducer, assaulting (male) continence as a sort of first principle of redeemed society. Here, as elsewhere, the Puritans could never come to the end of their own sexual *entendre*. And Hawthorne merely brought their language game to full sexual life.[28]

Yet the discovery of an exuberant life of Puritan sexual metaphor – now mystifying their own doctrine, now discrediting another's — may only serve to deepen our sense of how utterly insoluble, "puritanically," the case of Hester Prynne will prove. Any symbol system that turns out to be all tenor and no vehicle will not only produce awkward allegories, but may result, more seriously, in an impoverished vocabulary of life. And so it may well have been with the Puritans, those inveterate symbolizers of sex.

Although too complex to argue here, the historical formula may be simple enough: Taking natural life (too readily) for granted, Puritans valorize salvation and the life of grace; "coarse" enough (as Hawthorne suggests) about the ordinary details of coupling, pregnancy, and nurture, these eminent pre-Victorians turn all their subtlety to the "higher" task of discovering and organizing the typology by which such things *mean,* beyond themselves, in a decently spiritual way. Better to marry than to burn, clearly, for how could one on fire with fleshly lust successfully meditate the logic by which sex and marriage have been made types of the soul's closing with the heavenly bridegroom or of Christ's espousal of a truly virgin church? Yet where everything is already symbolic, the real world may have trouble finding its own language. Perhaps it will yet appear that the profound Puritan interest in the theological, ecclesiastic, and even political analogies of sex and marriage all but displaced their more literal curiosity and judgment. Possibly their metaphors obscured rather than redeemed their own sexual life.[29]

Here Dimmesdale — although without precedent in Winthrop — would seem to be the most obvious case. Although the casual reader may infer that his seven-year regimen of fleshly self-crucifixion is designed to pay back in pain what he once enjoyed of pleasure, the subtler evidence suggests that his real problem goes deeper and involves a theology less obvious than that of holy masochism. As I have argued elsewhere, more patiently, the unspoken premise of his "hypothetical" debate with Chillingworth about confession, and the last revelation of his somewhat franker discussion with Hester about repentance, both indicate that he is not so much haunted by the specter of remorse for a single (natural) sexual deviation as he is consumed by fear that his "adultery" is really a classic case of "idolatry" — that is, that he did once and does still love Hester more than God, preferring the creature to the creator in the one just definition of the unregenerate will. He tortures his flesh truly enough, but what torments him is an (Augustinian) allegory of saving faith.[30]

Indeed, what else *can* Dimmesdale be thinking when he tells Hester he has tried to persevere as a chosen saint but now accepts his doom and would even seal it by "snatch[ing] the solace allowed to the condemned culprit" (p. 201)? Social conscience he has seemed entirely to lack, weakly permitting Hester to bear the entire responsibility and burden of Pearl. And, since he has been ignorant all along of the sexual identity of Chillingworth, how could he attach so much significance to what his world all but dismissed — with a wave of the whip — as "single fornication"? Only by rejecting Hester utterly, in the end, can this thoroughgoing Puritan ideologue recover his lost, allegorical identity.

Here Hester's case seems simpler, more naturalistic and more truly sexual. When we determine to consider her *as herself,* rather than as some Hutchinson surrogate, we quickly notice that she feels shame, admits that she has wronged Chillingworth, loves Pearl (in spite of certain "monstrous" fears),[31] and wants to live with Dimmesdale; eventually she will propose they simply escape from the utopia that has allegorized the sexual and mystified the police force. Yet in the end, even this most natural of Hawthorne's protagonists is presented as a function of Puritan metaphor. A victim, if not an exponent. Which may be one powerful reason why naturalistic readers continue to identify with her, even after they are shown that the fiercely logical structure of *The Scarlet Letter* points to Dimmesdale as the indubitable center of literary organization.[32] Dimmesdale ably abets the (male) myth he suffers. Hester merely endures it, for seven years; then she nullifies it — although she may also, much later, return to sponsor a new one of her own.

The clearest revelation of Hester's metaphoric enclosure and eruption (and also, not incidentally, of Hawthorne's full debt to Winthrop's *Journal*) comes in her own emotional overflow in the famous forest scene. The force of the moment derives partly from the fact that, unlike almost everything else in that thoroughly prepared-for episode, the outburst comes as a surprise to both Hester and the reader. But also, partly, from the fact that Hester's silent thought seems to be echoing New England's single most powerful figure of social organization. We should proceed with caution.

For Hester's theory of paranuptial "consecration" (p. 195) and for her later, more energetic proposal of "trial and success" (p. 198) in a world elsewhere, the antinomian suggestions of "Another View of Hester" (Chapter 13) have fully prepared us. Her views horrify the narrator, of course. An accomplished reader of Winthrop, he no doubt considers her plan comparable to that of many other failed Puritans who had "crept out at a broken wall": one more rash assertion of some singular (or, more oddly, dual) "liberty" set against the terms of an earlier covenant of perfect mutuality founded on a holy love transcending both justice and mercy. Indeed, his evocation of the "untamed forest" as an apt figure of Hester's "moral wilderness" (p. 199) well recalls Winthrop's impassioned protest against the supposed logic of certain backsliders from his utopian society:

> For such as come together into a wilderness, where are nothing but wild beasts and beastlike men, and there confederate together in civil and church estate, whereby they do, implicitly at least, bind themselves to support each other, and all of them that society, whether civil or sacred, whereof they are members, how they can break from this without free consent, is hard to find, so as may satisfy a tender or good conscience in time of trial.[33]

Clearly, Dimmesdale himself has felt the force of this sentiment – daring not to "quit [his] post, though an unfaithful sentinel" (p. 197) on the walls separating (but metaphorically) the enclosed garden of New England from the wilderness of the World. But Hester, we know, is not going to be impressed.

Winthrop's "Model of Christian Charity" (which the narrator has blandly assimilated into "the world's law") is now "no law for her mind" (p. 164). Nor, given the ragged terms of her own migration to New England, can the reader entirely disagree. Unless it were when she decided to remain there, to be close to Dimmesdale, morbidly hoping for some "joint futurity of endless retribution" (p. 80), how had she, any more than Henry Thoreau, ever made a contract with the State of Massachusetts? Yet the surprise – and the full revelation of Winthrop – comes just earlier, in the aftermath of her disclosure of her long-concealed (second) secret, the identity of Chillingworth. Hardly more ashamed than out-raged, Dimmesdale splutters over "the indelicacy! – the horrible ugliness of this exposure" and, forgetting all he otherwise owes the "wondrous strength and generosity of [this] woman's heart" (p. 68), fiercely avows that he "cannot forgive" (p. 194) this one deception so crucial to their mutual conspiracy.[34] Yet he *does* for-give, as we feel he must. And the reason may have as much to do with the suppressed terms as with the "sudden and desperate tenderness" of Hester's impassioned plea.

She merely holds him fast, "lest he should look her sternly in the face." But the narrator appears to know the inevitable lan-guage of her silent thought:

> All the world had frowned on her, – for seven long years had it frowned upon this lonely woman, – and still she bore it all, nor ever once turned away her firm, sad eyes. Heaven, likewise, had frowned upon her, and she had not died. But the frown of this pale, weak, sinful, and sorrow-stricken man was what Hester could not bear, and live! (pp. 194–5)

Why the repeated stress on *frown*, we wonder. Can mere repetition possibly compensate the effect of a word *obviously* too weak to capture the force of Dimmesdale's violent energy of resentment? Or the allegorical outrage by which a covenanted community has implemented its unpardonable judgment of a pardonable sin? Or the theological injury of an infinite God? Yet it is just a *frown* that Hester's life cannot sustain. And the single word is sufficient to evoke the crucial context in Winthrop.

A figure of speech, of course, it nevertheless climaxes the tedious argument whose intent it was – insidious or not – to bind the souls of all his saintly citizens to the social compact they had entered. Therein was "liberty," but only such as "is maintained and exercised in a way of subjection to authority"; it was indeed the same "liberty wherewith Christ has made us free." Then, as if not content with this ultimate mystification (as Roger Williams would see it) of the mere exigencies of discipline in wilderness states and wilderness churches, Winthrop proceeds to suggest how it can all be perfectly naturalized in the typology of pauline mar-riage: "The woman's own choice makes such a man her hus-

New Essays on The Scarlet Letter

band," even as the soul must voluntarily enter the covenant of grace, or instituted church, or separated civil polity; "yet being so chosen, he is her lord, and she is subject to him, yet in a way of liberty, not of bondage," even as those who have espoused New England are now "subject" so freely. Indeed the "yoke" of this quasi-marital covenant is as "easy and sweet . . . as a bride's ornaments":

> and if through frowardness or wantonness, etc., she shake it off, at any time, she is at no rest in her spirit, until she take it up again; and whether her lord smiles upon her, and embraceth her in his arms, or whether he *frowns* or rebukes, or smites her, she apprehends the sweetness of his love in all, and is refreshed, supported, and instructed by every such dispensation of his authority over her.[35] (Italics added)

Just here, along with so much else, is the source of the frown that Hester cannot bear. Yet subversively redefined: The word is the word of Winthrop's Sovereign Lord, but the frown is the frown of Hester's fleshly lover.

The *literal* must pass without much notice: With or without the fortunate example of Milton's Eve, the liberated will scarcely admire the sociology of Puritan wedlock. Nor need we stress the obvious political tenor of Winthrop's "holy pretense": Contractual absolutism is absolutism still; and "how like an iron cage . . . "[36] Closer to Hawthorne's best ironic point would be Winthrop's prediction of the way Hester "shakes off" and then "takes up again" the letter (and the cap) that mark her subjection to some diffused but scarcely attenuated male authority – as if Pearl's own " 'Come thou and take it up' " (p. 210) were but one more (absurd) displacement of an ever-present Winthrop. Yet the emphasis rightly falls on the *frown*, the vital clue to the real terms of Hester's metaphorical bondage and effectual rebellion, and of Hawthorne's relentless deconstruction. State, church, and God himself may frown on Hester, but not Dimmesdale. Political gentlemen may have their pious little allegories, but "the woman's own choice," it finally appears, has made *this* man her *only* viable lord and husband. The rest is somebody else's quaint little language experiment – magical, as long as it works, but void whenever it does not. And just here, clearly, it does not, as even Dimmesdale may feel the silent force of Hester's idolatrous substitution of himself in the place of covenantal authority.

Ultimately the problem is not Chillingworth or any other casuistic instance in "The Doctrine and Discipline of Divorce." The problem is in the language, reduced to materialistic absurdity on the one side, only to be elevated to mystic overdetermination on the other. Dimmesdale's (Cottonesque) affair is with the Bridegroom of the (always female) Puritan soul; and the first love of the Puritan magistrates is always their own unadulterated system of symbols.[37] All men and — to be puritanically fair, at last — all women too will always be sinners in the flesh. Winthrop's Boston is decidedly not "perfectionistic" in the manner of Noyes's silversmooth Oneida. But how *can* Hester prefer Dimmesdale to God? Or, to be fairer still, to the terms that empower the Puritan utopia? Marriages are made by fools like Bellingham; but only God can make an Allegory. Which Hester here breaks.

At issue, all along, has been something beyond the more than Eve-like "frowardness" of Hester's unruly female sexuality, flaunted however literally in the "embroidery" of human art. Deeper down, all along, has lurked the problem of her imperfect subjection to the "easy and sweet authority" of those who teach that, under the terms of New England's special covenant, all valid human willing is but a "true wife," who "accounts her subjection her honor and freedom, and would not think her condition safe and free but in her subjection to . . . the authority of Christ, her king and husband." No wonder the narrator finds Hester's outward "humility" (p. 162) so dangerously deceptive; no wonder he portentously concludes that her "scarlet letter had not done its office" (p. 166). Its failure is clearly a failure of metaphor. For, given her "own choice," this woman *will* always choose her own literal lover before any version of Winthrop's figurative husband, even in hell. And Emily Dickinson herself could scarcely make the Puritan blasphemy more blatant.[38]

Hester may or may not continue to believe in the God whose "merciful" will Dimmesdale closes his earthly career by explicating with such meticulous orthodoxy. She certainly seems to believe, much later, in the coming of some new sexual morality, although not by her to be revealed. But what makes her guilty, in the view of the decidedly *un*liberated narrator, of a "deadlier crime than [the adultery] stigmatized by the scarlet letter" (p. 164) is her flat rejection of the metaphorical identity between the Pauline marriage and Winthrop's puritanic utopia — considered as, itself, "the redeemed form of man." Never is her effective choice between Roger Chillingworth and Arthur Dimmesdale; always it is between a human lover and the figure of salvation in covenant. Tempted all along to conform to the community's constituted disbelief in the validity of her sexual love for Dimmesdale, she seems nevertheless just waiting for the moment of her "own choice." And when it comes, she passionately chooses the literal. To which she *almost* converts even Dimmesdale. Apparently nature lurks, just waiting for our figures to fail.

5

The occasion of Winthrop's justly famous "little speech" on the quasi-marital nature of "liberty" and "authority" had been one more dispute — this time in 1645 — over the discretionary power of magistrates to intervene for order wherever the laws or precedents of a newly formed community seemed insufficiently precise to cover the singular human case. And thus it is probably worth noting that "Governor" Bellingham's own intervention into Hester's domestic situation also occurs in 1645, as historical critics plot the novel's fictional action against the background of actual time.[39] One more strategically ineffectual displacement of the definitive pretext: Hester's too casual stewardship is attacked and defended just when Winthrop's own was most authoritatively impugned and philosophically defended; a whole "way" really *is* up for grabs.

But the "sources" of *The Scarlet Letter* run deeper than the discovery of political confusion beneath the theocratic monolith. For Hester's ultimate rebellion is against a myth far older than that of puritanic consensus. One there from the outset; and written, as it must have seemed, in stone.

Even as his utopian "Model," Winthrop had implied that law was just like love, that civil combinations were but reflections of that more ideal union of man and woman. And nowhere more so than in the "City upon a Hill" his migrant Puritans were about to posit. That everywhere the citizen had to obey the magistrate might almost pass without saying, unless some proleptic disciple of D. H. Lawrence should suppose the moral of America was "Henceforth be masterless." What needed stressing, apparently, was the theological guarantee and, even more so, the precise quality of that obedience in a Bible state. As a member "of Christ," the citizen his rhetoric hoped to create would discern "his own Image and resemblance in another, and therefore cannot but love him as he loves himself"; self-love, if one insists, but redeemed by the recognition that ultimately the true self is always Christ.[40] And thus redeemed, what possibly frustrates an overflowing abundance of love among the members?

Probably the reader of *The Scarlet Letter* should read the full text of the loving outburst that follows, for Hawthorne seems to have recognized it as Winthrop's own theme song for New England:

> It is like Adam when Eve was brought to him; shee must have it one with herselfe: this is fleshe of my fleshe (saith shee) and bone of my bone; shee conceives a great delighte in it, therefore shee desires nearenes and familiarity with it. Shee hath a greate propensity to doe it good and receives such content in it; as fearing the miscarriage of her beloved, shee bestowes it in the inmost closett of her heart; shee will not endure that it shall want any good which shee can give it. If by occasion shee by withdrawne from the Company of it, shee is still lookeing towardes the place where shee left her beloved, if shee heare it groane shee is with it presently; if shee finde it sadd and disconsolate shee sighes and mournes with it, shee hath noe such joy, as to see her beloved merry and thriveing; if shee see it wronged, shee cannot beare it without passion. Shee setts noe boundes of her affeccions, nor hath any thought of reward, shee findes recompence enoughe in the exercise of her love towardes it.[41] (Punctuation added)

Winthrop may go on to point the moral in the biblical example of Jonathan and David, considered as eminent (if typic) "Christians." But we notice rather that the spiritual point of view is indeed female; that the fervent rhetoric (here) stops just short of predicting Eve's response to an Adamic "frown"; and that in fact it characterizes nothing quite so well as what Dimmesdale rightly calls the "Wondrous strength and generousity of a woman's heart" (p. 68). As if Winthrop were bidding to become a sort of theological feminist.

Yet the passage is altogether metaphorical: The love is the love of the citizen, under the law; or, in the extreme case, made *painfully* explicit after fifteen years of "libertine" experiment and "constitutional" wrangling, of the saintly citizen *for* the law. Just here is the enthusiastic premise of Winthrop's more than lawyerly vision of holy order in New England – our excuse for treating him as more than a mere magistrate, Hawthorne's justification for calling his Boston a "Utopia of human virtue" (p. 47), and Hester's ultimate reason for rebellion. The distinguishing mark of Winthrop's New World citizen-saint was precisely his (or, should the case ever arise, her) renewed spiritual ability to love the law as the unfallen Eve had once so fully loved the mated partner of her own Edenic soul; or, as the figure takes its final winged flight, as the liberated soul will always love its saving Christ, that one promiscuous bridegroom-lover of all truly gracious souls.

A cynicism suggests itself at once, of course: Winthrop's vaunted "liberty" of law-like-love will actually entitle the saintly citizens of New England to do no other than "those things that qualified magistrates . . . and learned clergymen" would say they might.[42] But as long as rhetoric matters at all, it is surely worth noticing that Winthrop begins the Massachusetts experiment sounding as much like an arch-enthusiast as like a perfect Tory. And no American Puritan ever gave either a more lyrical or yet a more technical expression of Boston's oddly unpuritanic variety of sexual politics – neither poets like Bradstreet and Taylor nor theologians like Cotton and Shepard. Always female, the soul of "man" is the subject of one adequate passion, whose sole object is the Divine Other that is Christ; and which, if it does *not* feel, all the rest is legalism surely. Or repression. Or force.[43]

Yet it is not quite cynicism (but merely adequacy to the various dystopian texts of history) to notice that it did not quite work out. Winthrop's *Journal* itself records – ruefully, if not bitterly – the more obvious human failures to meet his holy terms: the antinomian divorce of grace from law on the one side and the altogether loveless quarrel about civil rights on the other. All of which forced him to repeat, for the record, the less lovely side of his complex

126

original thought: "if you will be satisfied to enjoy" such liberties "as Christ allows you, then you will quietly submit unto that authority which is set over you, in all the administrations of it, for your good."[44] Even as Hester Prynne's seven-year submission manages to persuade everyone (except the narrator of her tale) that she is only too willing to do. Until her final rebellion, when her "sudden and desperate" seizing of Dimmesdale convinces us that her own text implies a rejection of Winthrop's terms altogether. The law, say the lawyers, is the law; but love involves "a consecration of its own."

It would be too much, doubtless, to suggest that *The Scarlet Letter* fully endorses *this* particular form of antinomian rebellion, which shocks the narrator almost as much as it does Dimmesdale. His "'Hush, Hester!'" (p. 195) speaks well enough for the civil reader's sense that local customs of courtship, marriage, and divorce are at least as complex and subject to social regulation as Winthrop had sensed, whatever Bellingham may have thought. Thus, the "novel of adultery" – not to mention the more ambitious project of "deceit, desire, and the novel" – will surely survive the worst that Hester's rebellion (or Hawthorne's deconstruction) can possibly accomplish. But it is only fair, and indeed it is somehow necessary, to recognize that Hester's case is not entirely sociological, nor even altogether ethical. Her choice, throughout *The Scarlet Letter* is never effectively between one human lover and another. Always it is between certain terms of complex socialization that have been mystically equated with the One Love no soul is free to reject and the passional motions of her own female temperament. An unforced option, surely.[45]

Even if it is, theologically speaking, quite like the one Dimmesdale in the end accepts – fleeing from the arms of Hester Prynne to those of the heavenly bridegroom his own (rather too feminine) nature finally manages to prefer. Obviously, though ironically, his decision turns out to be quite easy: all he has to accomplish is the identification of his true self (or soul) as the part of him that really does love his own (Calvinistic) idea of God's "name" and "His will" (p. 257) more than anything else, including Hester, whose fleshly existence his own flesh has found such an idolatrous temptation. Not quite so easy, perhaps, as it would be were he simply a

Platonist, fleeing "to the Fatherland" from the wiles of the Aphrodite of generation; for then his soul could remain a masculist after all. But easy enough, as it turns out, for even the *Christian* allegory was made by men; and arguably for the same (Platonic) purpose of escaping "the woman," by becoming her themselves. Not physiologically, of course, but allegorically, by "submission."

Evidently it is not so much "right" as it is inevitable that Hester will regret her own version of this sexually mysterious option. Or at least that she will frankly question, at the end, whether Dimmesdale's authentically (and apocalyptically) Puritan solution is indeed "better" (p. 256). For to whom, after all, ought she just now submit? Hardly to Dimmesdale, for he never has been her husband, and it would be only a little cruel to suggest that he is dying to evade that very role. Surely not to Chillingworth, whom not even Winthrop would dare regard as a type of Christ. And where is the critic who will propose submission to the Puritan community? – which never has known exactly what it was talking about. Besides, she has Pearl to consider: better, perhaps, if "we may both die, and little Pearl with us" (p. 254); otherwise it's all too confusing. Evidently the allegory works better for men than for women, whatever John Milton may have thought.[46] And evidently it is easier to be a woman allegorically than really.

Dimmesdale's "bright dying eyes" may indeed look "far into eternity" to see God, but Hester foresees only further years of single parenthood. Nor is her past of any present theological use. Her choice of Chillingworth – if choice it could be called – had not concealed, and could not be made to stand for, her prevenient willingness to accept only such liberty "as Christ allows." Nor could her "adultery" – as it after the fact turned out to be – possibly be construed as a whoring after strange gods. Dimmesdale dies believing he must choose "Hester or God," like some timid version of Melville's Pierre. Hester can only live on, finding time to return to some less utopian New England, free to consider again the proper "terms" of the human sexual relation. Hester "endures" (in Faulkner's sense) to rethink the problem of Hawthorne's "sources," in a world where even the best made metaphors eventually reveal themselves as such. Even if this means only that new ones must be made, in the space that always separates the soul from any supposable object of its own desire.[47]

NOTES

1 The standard source study of *The Scarlet Letter* (SL) is Charles Ryskamp, "The New England Sources of SL," *American Literature* 31 (1959): 257–72. Its final, modest claim is for "A firm dependence upon certain New England histories for the background of *The Scarlet Letter*" (271).

2 See my own "Footsteps of Ann Hutchinson: The Context of SL," *ELH* 39 (1972), esp. 466–85.

3 For the three issues in question see, respectively, Ryskamp, "New England Sources," 260–1, 267; Ernest W. Baughman, "Public Confession and SL," *New England Quarterly* 40 (1967): 532–50; and Michael Davitt Bell, *Hawthorne and the Historical Romance of New England* (Princeton, N.J.: Princeton University Press, 1971), pp. 135–7.

4 Arguing against the relevance of Puritanism to much of America's classic literature, William C. Spengemann concedes Winthrop as an "apparent" source of SL but writes off the pursuit of such matters as "a harmless provincialism"; see his "Review Essay," *Early American Literature* 16 (1981): 184–5. It may yet appear, however, that Winthrop is more nearly Hawthorne's vital subject than his necessary source.

5 This study cautiously proposes that one take seriously the suggestion of the first chapter of SL – that its historical world should indeed be regarded as some projected "Utopia of human virtue and happiness" (47). An analysis of Hawthorne's reduction of utopian pretense to local ideology might well base itself on Fredric Jameson's "Dialectic of Utopia and Ideology," in *The Political Unconscious* (Ithaca, N.Y.: Cornell University Press, 1981), pp. 281–99.

6 Although three years of real or "maturational" time have elapsed when Hester is called from her needle to appear before Governor Bellingham, the "fictional" time is brief indeed. This successful manipulation of dramatic or psychic time contributes to the novel's brilliant compression and marks Hawthorne's narrative advance over his longer tales (e.g., "The Gentle Boy"); see my own *Province of Piety* (Cambridge: Harvard University Press, 1984), esp. pp. 179–81.

7 For the "worthy" observation on the puritanic sensitivities of mice, see *Winthrop's Journal: "History of New England,"* ed. J. K. Hosmer, vol. II (New York: Scribners, 1908), p. 18.

8 See Ryskamp, "New England Sources," 265. For Morison's discussion of the transformation of the Massachusetts charter into a workable constitution – including his account of "the *cause célèbre* of Goody Sherman and her stray sow" – see *Builders of the Bay Colony* (Boston: Houghton Mifflin, 1930), pp. 83–94; cf. George Lee Haskins, *Law and Authority in Early Massachusetts* (New York: Macmillan, 1960), esp. pp. 9–65; and Edwin Powers, *Crime and Punishment in Early Massachusetts* (Boston: Beacon Press, 1966), esp. pp. 45–99.

9 For Winthrop's original account of the stray sow, see *Journal*, vol. II, pp. 64–6; for the political aftermath, see *Journal*, vol. II, pp. 211–17. Dating the action of SL has proved simple enough: Pearl is seven years old by the end of the story, which the text itself marks as 1649 by its mention of the death of Governor Winthrop; it thus begins in 1642 and, as the narrative declares, "in this month of June" (p. 48); see Ryskamp, "New England Sources," 259–61.

10 Winthrop, *Journal*, vol. I, p. 305.

11 See Robert Emmet Wall, Jr., *Massachusetts Bay: The Crucial Decade, 1640–1650* (New Haven, Conn.: Yale University Press, 1972), esp. pp. 41–92.

12 See Ryskamp, "New England Sources," 260, 267–68; cf. Bell, *Historical Romance*, pp. 135–6.

13 For the view that Hawthorne's recent political experiences figure largely in the dramatic action of SL itself, see James R. Mellow, *Nathaniel Hawthorne in His Times* (Boston: Houghton Mifflin, 1980), esp. pp. 292–308; and also, much more radically, Stephen Nissenbaum, Introduction to *The Scarlet Letter and Selected Writings* (New York: Modern Library, 1984), esp. pp. xix–xxxvi.

14 *Journal*, vol. II, pp. 43–4; the entry is for Nov. 8, 1642. For a brief review of the (sparsely preserved) facts of Bellingham's life, see the article by Henry P. Stearns in the *Dictionary of American Biography*, vol. II, ed. Allen Johnson (New York: Scribners, 1927), pp. 166–7; cf. James Savage, *A Genealogical Dictionary of the First Settlers of New England* (Boston: Little, Brown, 1860), pp. 161–2.

15 The editorial remark is that of Hosmer: see Winthrop, *Journal*, vol. II, p. 44. See also John Gorham Palfrey, *History of New England*, Vol. I (London: Longman, 1849), pp. 611–12.

16 The references are, respectively, *The Bourgeois Experience: Victoria to Freud* (New York: Oxford University Press, 1984); and *The History of*

Sexuality, tr. Robert Hurley (New York: Vintage Books, 1980). For the argument that Hawthorne's Puritans *already* typify this modern (bourgeois) world, see Charles Feidelson, Jr., "The Scarlet Letter," in Roy Harvey Pearce, ed., *Hawthorne Centenary Essays* (Columbus: Ohio State University Press, 1964), pp. 31–77.

17 Granting the specific 1642–9 setting of SL, a few critics have thought to ask, "why just *then?*" But the answers have largely centered on events in England. H. Bruce Franklin neatly evokes the situations of Bellingham and Winthrop, but turns quickly to the context of the English Civil War; see his Introduction to *The Scarlet Letter and Other Writings by Nathaniel Hawthorne* (Philadelphia: Lippincott, 1967), pp. 13–17. See also Frederick Newberry, "Tradition and Disinheritance in *The Scarlet Letter*," *ESQ* 23 (1977): 1–26.

18 For the expurgated materials, see the James Savage edition of John Winthrop, *The History of New England from 1630 to 1649*, vol. II (Boston: Phelps and Farnham, 1825–6), pp. 45–50. For Hawthorne's knowledge of this edition, see Marion L. Kesselring, *Hawthorne's Reading* (New York: New York Public Library, 1949), p. 64.

19 Winthrop, *Journal* (Hosmer ed.), Vol. II, p. 38.

20 Winthrop, *Journal* (Savage ed.), Vol. II, p. 46.

21 It is virtually impossible, of course, that Hawthorne could have seen the Bradford text itself, since it had disappeared from (private) circulation since the Revolution and was not printed until 1856. Nor, significantly, do any of the historians who loyally retell parts of his story (often verbatim) include any mention of the "wickedness" that totally preoccupied his attention in 1642. Yet his own account powerfully reinforces the impression created by Winthrop – of a whole godly nation frightfully astounded by an unseemly return of the repressed; and the "answers" he includes indelibly reinscribe the painful terms of the Bellingham questionnaire as described by Winthrop. To read Bradford into the record is thus merely to authenticate Hawthorne's primary intuition. For the history of the text in question, see Samuel Eliot Morison's Introduction to William Bradford, *Of Plymouth Plantation* (New York: Knopf, 1952), pp. xxvii–xxxii. For Bradford's (interwoven) account of "wickedness" at both Plymouth and Massachusetts Bay, see pp. 316–22; for the answers the Plymouth elders gave to Bellingham, see pp. 404–13.

22 See Winthrop, *Journal* (Savage ed.), vol. II, p. 47; cf. Bradford, *Plymouth*, pp. 404, 407, 408–12. In fairness, it should be pointed out that, although the defendants in question escaped with severe whippings, confinements, and social brandings, the case eventually forced a clear

definition of rape and a declaration that in the future it would be a capital offense – despite the lack of warrant from the Scriptures. See Haskins, *Law and Authority*, pp. 116, 150–151; cf. Powers, *Crime and Punishment*, pp. 264–8.

23 Winthrop, *Journal* (Savage ed.), Vol. II, p. 47; and Bradford, *Plymouth*, p. 318.

24 It should go without saying that Hawthorne had noticed the case of "one Mary Latham," put to death for her adultery (with James Britton), but only after this "once proper young woman" taunted the husband of her loveless marriage as "old rogue and cockold"; see Winthrop, *Journal* (Hosmer ed.), vol. II, pp. 161–3.

25 The quotation is from Faulkner's "Delta Autumn." For a brief selection of John Winthrop's letters to (and from) his (third) wife, Margaret, see Perry Miller and Thomas H. Johnson, eds., *The Puritans*, vol. II (New York: Harper & Row, 1963), pp. 465–571; as the editors remark, these letters "reveal certain depths of the Puritan spirit and the nature of conjugal affection in Puritan households" (p. 464).

26 See John Cotton, *A Brief Exposition . . . Upon the Whole Book of Canticles* (London: Ralph Smith, 1755), esp. pp. 4–8; this rare edition has been reprinted, in facsimile, as a volume of the Research Library of Americana (New York: Arno Press, 1972). For the (sexual) implication of Cotton in SL, see my own "Footsteps," esp. pp. 486–94.

27 Cotton's "standard catechism for New England children" bore the title: *Spiritual Milk for Boston Babes In Either England, Drawn out of the Breasts of Both Testaments*; see David Leverenz, *The Language of Puritan Feeling* (New Brunswick, N.J.: Rutgers University Press, 1980), p. 2. Leverenz's (psychoanalytic) study amply documents the Puritans' widespread use of sexual language for a variety of "higher" concerns. On the crucial question of "weaned affections," see Perry Miller, *The New England Mind: The Seventeenth Century* (Cambridge, Mass.: Harvard University Press, 1939), pp. 35–63; and Edmund S. Morgan, *The Puritan Family* (New York: Harper & Row, 1966), pp. 29–86.

28 See Colacurcio, "Footsteps," esp. 470–8.

29 For an unhysterical modern account of the Puritans' *real* difficulties with sexuality – beneath both their coarseness and their metaphoric enthusiasm – see Philip Greven, *The Protestant Temperament* (New York: Alfred A. Knopf, 1977), esp. pp. 62–73, 124–48. The opposite (or at least a more forgiving) view is advanced by Robert Daly, *God's Altar* (Berkeley: University of California Press, 1978), esp. pp. 26–7.

30 See Colacurcio, "Footsteps," 490–3.

31 As I have shown elsewhere, Hester's habit of looking fearfully, day

after day, into Pearl's "expanding nature," constantly expecting "to detect some dark and wild peculiarity" (p. 90) plainly echoes the Puritans' ascription of Ann Hutchinson's "monster birth" to her heresies; see "Footsteps," 476–7.

32 Structural analysis of SL always points to the definitive importance of the three scaffold scenes at precisely the beginning, middle, and end of the novel's drama. Such an approach must always privilege Dimmesdale: When (and why) will he eventually get up where he belongs, in the naked light of day? See Leland Schubert, *Hawthorne the Artist* (Chapel Hill: University of North Carolina Press, 1944), pp. 137–8.

33 Winthrop, *Journal* (Hosmer ed.), vol. II, pp. 83–4.

34 Ironically, Dimmesdale decides to run away with Hester the very day he discovers she still has a living husband. The point was first seized upon (somewhat too moralistically) by Robert F. Haugh, "The Second Secret in SL," *College English* 17 (1956): 269–71.

35 Winthrop, *Journal* (Hosmer ed.), vol. II, pp. 238–9.

36 Such is the verdict on Puritan "liberty" in Hawthorne's sketch called "Main Street," published the year before SL and alluded to in "The Custom-House": "How like an iron cage was that which they called Liberty!" See the Centenary Edition of *The Snow Image and Uncollected Tales* (Columbus: Ohio State University Press, 1974), p. 58. The *allusion*, as Q. D. Leavis long ago pointed out, is almost certainly to the place in *The Pilgrim's Progress* where "Christian is shown a man in an iron cage as an awful example of what a true Christian should never be"; see "Hawthorne as Poet," reprinted in A. N. Kaul, ed., *Hawthorne: A Collection of Critical Studies* (Englewood Cliffs, N.J.: Prentice-Hall, 1966), p. 35. The *reference*, however, is just as surely to Winthrop's representative and famous "little speech." For an extended consideration of Winthrop's political thought, see Loren Baritz, "Political Theology," in *City on a Hill* (New York: Wiley, 1964), pp. 3–45; cf. G. L. Mosse, *The Holy Pretense* (New York: Howard Fertig, 1968), pp. 88–106.

37 Conveniently, the case of Thomas Shepard may be added to those of the semiantinomian John Cotton, the Canticles-inspired Edward Taylor, and the decidedly female Anne Bradstreet to suggest that Puritan men and women thought of their souls alike, allegorically, as female: Shepard's conversion clearly involved his accepting Christ as "Husband"; see his *Autobiography*, edited by Michael McGiffert as *God's Plot* (Amherst: University of Massachusetts Press, 1974), p. 45. For the generality of the phenomenon, see "Brides of Christ" in Greven, *Protestant Temperament*, pp. 124–48. On the other hand, for the Puritans'

"liberal" divorce policy, see Emil Oberholzer, *Delinquent Saints* (New York: Columbia University Press, 1956), pp. 117–18.

38 For the relevant "blasphemy" of Emily Dickinson, see "I cannot live with you," in Thomas H. Johnson, ed., *Final Harvest* (Boston: Little, Brown, 1961), pp. 162–4.

39 See Franklin, *SL and Other Writings*, p. 15.

40 John Winthrop, "Model of Christian Charity," *Collections of the Massachusetts Historical Society*, 3rd Series, vol. VII, 1838, p. 42. For the "true" identity of the Puritan self, see Sacvan Bercovitch, *The Puritan Origins of the American Self* (New Haven, Conn.: Yale University Press, 1975), esp. pp. 1–34. And for D. H. Lawrence's moral of America, see *Studies in Classic American Literature* (reprint Garden City, N.Y.: Doubleday, 1951), pp. 11–18.

41 Winthrop, "Model"; quoted from the corrected text of Edmund S. Morgan, ed., *Puritan Political Ideas* (Indianapolis: Bobbs-Merrill, 1965), pp. 87–8. For Hawthorne's knowledge of the 1838 version, (cited above), see Colacurcio, *Piety*, pp. 237, 597.

42 See Perry Miller, ed., *The Puritans* (Garden City, N.Y.: Doubleday, 1956), p. 90.

43 Both of Miller's widely used anthologies truncate Winthrop's "Model" badly, eliding both its theology and its sexual metaphors, and thus stressing instead its arch-conservative theory of social hierarchy; see, for example, Miller and Johnson, *Puritans*, pp. 195–202. This simplified version of the original vision tends to reinforce the decidedly partial view of Winthrop as altogether secular and lawyerly; see Vernon L. Parrington, *Main Currents in American Thought* (New York: Harcourt, Brace, 1927), pp. 38–50; cf. Darrett B. Rutman, *Winthrop's Boston* (Chapel Hill: University of North Carolina Press, 1965), esp. pp. 19–21.

44 Winthrop, *Journal* (Hosmer ed.), vol. II, p. 239.

45 David Leverenz rightly denies that Hawthorne ultimately "reduces Hester's radical perceptions to her sexuality," but his psychosexual reading fails (in my view) to identify the metaphorical (theological) burden of that sexuality; see "Mrs. Hawthorne's Headache: Reading *The Scarlet Letter*," *Nineteenth-Century Fiction* 37 (1983): 552–75. For the larger novelistic traditions in question, see Judith Armstrong, *The Novel of Adultery* (London: Macmillan, 1976); Tony Tanner, *Adultery in the Novel* (Baltimore: Johns Hopkins University Press, 1979); and, much more philosophically, René Girard, *Deceit, Desire, and the Novel*, tr. Yvonne Freccero (Baltimore: Johns Hopkins University Press, 1965).

46 The infamous formula of *Paradise Lost* — "Hee for God only, shee for God in him" (Book IV, line 299) — clearly implies that woman's "natural" sex role makes her theological submission seem natural as well. The logic of SL would seem to question that implication.

47 Although Melville's literary response to Hawthorne is the most famous such case in all of American literary history, the influence of SL has been remarkably difficult to detect. Restoring the emphasis on metaphoric sexuality makes its link to *Pierre* (1852) seem obvious and powerful. It may also indicate that Melville read Dimmesdale as a precursor of the sort of "feminization" that appears to have marked the nineteenth century; see Ann Douglas, *The Feminization of American Culture* (New York: Alfred A. Knopf, 1977), esp. pp. 80–117, 294–6, 309–13. It is also imaginable that, granting a certain theological slippage, Dimmesdale's death-by-allegory predicts the sexual attenuation of Quentin Compson.

His Folly, Her Weakness: Demystified Adultery in *The Scarlet Letter*

CAROL BENSICK

Hawthorne's distinctive emphasis on the historical context of moral and psychological experience has somewhat obscured *The Scarlet Letter*'s generic affinities. Yet there is evident weight in Q. D. Leavis's suggestion, in her classic 1951 essay "Hawthorne as Poet," that "the just comparison with *The Scarlet Letter* is . . . *Anna Karenina*."[1] For Hawthorne's tale discovers the same traditional pattern, recurrent in the European novel since Madame de La Fayette's *Princesse de Clèves* (1678), that Tolstoy's own novel regards.

But while "the novel of adultery"[2] is evidently *The Scarlet Letter*'s most appropriate genre, studious comparison of Hawthorne and Tolstoy uncovers a basic anomaly in Hawthorne's relation to their mutual tradition. The classic script, while deploring society's gratuitous tormenting of the adulteress, nevertheless assumes misery to be her unavoidable portion; thus *Anna Karenina*, without otherwise concerning itself with Mosaic law, assumes that somehow "the Lord . . . will repay" an unfaithful wife. Over the course of *The Scarlet Letter*, by contrast, the issue of extramarital sex (which Hawthorne conscientiously avoids labeling "adultery") makes a slow transition from the sphere of mystery to the sphere of marital sociology: No longer a fateful tragedy to be ritually suffered, adultery emerges as a practical human problem that the individuals involved have, along with their society, a common obligation to address.

1

Comparison with the example of Tolstoy verifies Hawthorne's command of the central elements of the tradition of literary adultery. Beneath the surface, the seventeenth-century Puritan marriage of Hawthorne's middle-class Anglo-Saxons incorporates the same basic elements as the nineteenth-century Eastern Orthodox union of Tolstoy's upper-class Russians. Like Aleksey Aleksandrovich Karenin, Roger Chillingworth is considerably older than his wife, and the match, like Karenin's, is an economic arrangement he contracted with her legal guardians. By themselves these factors might seem merely "historical," but by adding, like Tolstoy, the further provision that a vibrantly passionate, sensuous woman has been given to an exceptionally cold and undemonstrative man, Hawthorne sets the stage for the classic literary adultery.

A look at Anna quickly confirms Hester Prynne's proper literary context. Anna is a typical literary adulteress in not having been, before the advent of a suitor, unbearably dissatisfied with married life. Indeed, like the Princesse de Clèves, Anna feels a certain fondness for the older man to whom her relatives sold her girlhood: She "knew [a particular] characteristic in her husband, and liked it."[3] But at Karenin's customary initiation of conjugal lovemaking "with a meaningful smile," and the words, " 'It's time, it's time' " (AK, p. 119), she has, in the classic manner of the literary adulteress, learned to freeze.

Anna's reactions after commencing her affair with Vronsky are also typical. In the fashion of Emma Bovary, the literary adulteress classically attempts to transfer the burden of her afflicted conscience onto the provoking shortcomings of her husband.[4] Anna, comically using Aleksey Aleksandrovich's protruding ears as a pretext, nurses along her sexual indifference to him until it escalates into "a torturing sensation of physical loathing" (AK, p. 446). When Karenin finally confronts her, Anna justifies herself by projecting backward into the past feelings produced by the present situation: " 'I can't bear you, I'm afraid of you, and I hate you' " (AK, p. 225). Overtly, Anna grants that she is " 'a wicked woman, a lost woman' " (AK, p. 220); but in her heart, like Emma Bovary before her, she holds that her husband's intolerable ways exonerate her.

The "generic" elements reproduced in *Anna Karenina* – the wife's apparent content, her sexual incompatibility with her husband, and her final defensive claim of hatred – appear just as clearly in *The Scarlet Letter*. Even the young Hester Prynne was not deceived into thinking that "the utmost passion of her heart" (TSL, p. 176) had been awakened by her husband; when Chillingworth surprises her in the prison immediately after her public ordeal, she reminds him that she " 'was frank' " at their marriage: " 'I felt no love, nor feigned any' " (TSL, p. 74). Yet when Hester is enduring her punishment on the scaffold, the only clear flaw she recalls in her life with her husband ("a man well stricken in years," whose figure, Hester's "womanly fancy failed not to recall, was slightly deformed") was that it was "feeding itself on time-worn materials, like a tuft of green moss on a crumbling wall" (TSL, p. 58).

Seven years later, however, after her momentous talk with Chillingworth on the seashore announcing her intention to unmask him to Dimmesdale, Hester suffers a violent revulsion of feeling. Although in their actual conversation she had at least affected to agree that he had been " 'wise and just' " before she " 'made' " him " 'a fiend,' " she now glowers after him, dwelling morbidly on his "deformity," and says aloud, "bitterly," " 'Be it sin or not, I hate the man.' " Like Anna, Hester in typical literary adulteress fashion ultimately decides that her deepest feeling for her husband is hatred.

In a self-conscious attempt to soften her wicked feelings, Hester goes on to call up memories of her marriage; but although "such scenes had once appeared not otherwise than happy, now, as viewed through the dismal medium of her subsequent life, they classed themselves among her ugliest remembrances." Just as Anna feeds her righteous disgust at Aleksey Aleksandrovich's swollen knuckles, so Hester focuses on Chillingworth's humped shoulder. In an ecstasy of indulged revulsion, Hester "marvelled how such scenes could have been! She marvelled how she could ever have been wrought upon to marry him!" And as Hawthorne spells out what Tolstoy only hints, worst of all to Hester at this point is the idea that "she had ever endured, and reciprocated, the lukewarm grasp of his hand, and had suffered the smile of her lips and eyes to mingle and melt into his own" (TSL, p. 176).

Without analyzing it, the novel of adultery had established the tendency of the literary adulteress to identify her lover, as Emma does Rodolphe, as her true husband, while viewing her husband as a sort of violator.[5] Not content simply to document this classic phenomenon, Hawthorne goes on to articulate its basis. Hester's reactions make clear that what sets up the adulteress's classic inability to see her adultery as "her crime most to be repented of" is the original sexual incompatibility between the husband and wife. Because of her revulsion for her husband, that title is reserved for her wifely acquiescence.[6] From Hester's point of view, "it seemed a fouler offense committed by Roger Chillingworth, than any that had since been done him, that, in the time when her heart knew no better, he persuaded her to fancy herself happy at his side." Her adultery, Hester feels, was a crime only against church and state, but her submission to Chillingworth was an outrage she committed against herself. Thus, the reason the adulteress always concludes "Yes, I hate him," Hawthorne shows, is that she deeply believes "He betrayed me!" (TSL, p. 176).

For his part, Tolstoy too acknowledges that the adulteress's marriage was ill made; indeed, he permits one of his characters to spell out the original error. Anna's brother Stiva tells her, " 'You married a man twenty years older than yourself. You married him without love, not knowing what love was. It was a mistake, let's say' " (AK, p. 449). By contrast with Hawthorne, however, Tolstoy undercuts this rational interpretation by putting it into the mouth of a character elsewhere established as a philanderer. To discredit the position yet further, Tolstoy goes on to stipulate that Stiva experiences a pang of "conscience" while articulating this position: the voice of Jiminy Cricket warning him that, regarding marriage, a rational approach is "wrong" (AK, p. 440). In general, although the novelistic tradition always allowed that the adulteress had been the victim of a mismatch,[7] it was left to Hawthorne to draw an inference from that fact.

Overall, although both *The Scarlet Letter* and *Anna Karenina* visibly attend the same tradition of the incompatible marriage, the two novels' implicit interpretations of this literary phenomenon sharply diverge. Tolstoy's summary comment on all of Anna's shifts is this: Anna recalled "Aleksey Aleksandrovich as she spoke, with all the peculiarities of his figure and manner of speaking, and setting against him every defect she could find in him, softening nothing for the great wrong she was doing him" (AK, p. 201). Although Tolstoy often shows great sentimental pity for Anna herself, he passes unflinching judgment upon her actions. By contrast, although he is rather hard on Hester personally (hinting that Boston comes to show her "a more benign countenance . . . than she deserved" [p. 163]), the narrator of *The Scarlet Letter* sees inevitability, if not positive justice, in her position. Indeed, his most general reflection bears, if anything, less on the guilty wife than it does on the husband who went knowingly ahead with a misalliance:

> Let men tremble to win the hand of woman, unless they win along with it the utmost passion of her heart! Else it may be their miserable fortune, as it was Roger Chillingworth's, when some mightier touch than their own may have awakened all her sensibilities, to be reproached even for the calm content, the marble image of happiness which they will have imposed upon her as the warm reality. (TSL, pp. 176–7)

Where Tolstoy so insists on the idiosyncrasies of the characters in his adulterous triangle that it becomes finally impossible to draw any general conclusions from their individual lives, the experience of the members of Hawthorne's triangle distills itself into a pattern that *The Scarlet Letter* convinces us can be stated, however wryly, as something like a law. Which the novelistic tradition had not perfectly observed.

2

"Had Hester sinned alone?" asks the narrator of *The Scarlet Letter*. Of course not; and as the literary adulteress was not alone in her "sin," so is she also not alone in her suffering. Where there is an adulteress, there must of force be a cuckold; and although the whole tradition of the novel of adultery is witness to the predictable course of his behavior,[8] to untangle the feelings behind it was left to Hawthorne uniquely.

Typically a man of substance and standing in his community, the literary cuckold bases his reaction to his wife's infidelity on the assumption that he can be perfectly rational about it. Indeed, the typical cuckold is accustomed to assume he is exempt from merely emotional reactions altogether. Aleksey Aleksandrovich Karenin believes that because, as he thinks, " 'I am not to blame,' " it follows that, in his formulation, " 'I cannot suffer' " (AK, p. 299). Almost parodying this pattern, Roger Chillingworth even convinces himself that he would proceed with tormenting Dimmesdale " 'only for the art's sake' " (TSL, p. 138). If this were true, Chillingworth would indeed be, as he comes to fear, a fiend. As Hawthorne portrays him, however, the cuckold is only a self-deluded man, whose mistaken belief in his own disinterestedness sadly puts the seal on his fundamental misunderstanding with his wife.

Roger Chillingworth's successive reactions to the revelation of his wife's infidelity are clinically charted. Where Tolstoy needs to have his narrator step in to explain that Aleksey Aleksandrovich is really "profoundly miserable" (AK, p. 214), we witness Chillingworth's reactions on his face. As he watches Hester from the crowd, Chillingworth's features "darken" with a "convulsion" of "powerful emotion." It is only "by an effort of his will" that he achieves the calm expression, finger on lips, that Hester herself sees. Although it is integral to the tragedy that Hester cannot know this, Hawthorne makes clear to us that Chillingworth has not gotten over his "horror." His feelings have only "subsided into the depths of his nature" (TSL, p. 61).

That the cuckold is concealing his emotions and not, as his wife thinks, failing to experience any is a crucial provision in Hawthorne's analysis of literary adultery. Anna is typical in her supposition that Aleksey Aleksandrovich is " 'not a man, but a machine, and a spiteful machine' " (AK, p. 201), who simply " 'doesn't care' " what she does because he " 'doesn't know what love is' " (AK, p. 156). But by Chillingworth's reaction in the crowd, *The Scarlet Letter* shows that this assumption by the adulteress is a mistake. Unhappily, it is a mistake the cuckold characteristically does everything to foster.

As *Madame Bovary* makes plain, it is in the adulteress's long-standing assumption that her husband simply lacks feelings that her discontent begins.[9] But by his typical pretense to experience no emotional reaction even to infidelity, the classic cuckold effec-

142

tively confirms her error; if he fails to react to *that*, then surely nothing she can do will move him. The "Recognition" scene between Hester and Chillingworth is a graphic illustration of this tragicomic pattern. Catching sight of Chillingworth only after he has already arranged his face – missing the "convulsion" of his "horror" but getting the full offensive effect of his shushing finger – Hester, who like Anna habitually assumes that anyone who does not express feelings exactly the same way she does must not have any, is all but forced to conclude that his *only* reaction to herself, letter, and baby is a frigid concern for his good name.

Midway through *Anna Karenina*, Aleksey Aleksandrovich tells his wife that her betrayal has caused him " 'thuffering' " (AK, 384); without ever having him make so overt a profession, Hawthorne yet conveys Chillingworth's identical cuckold's pain. It is with a "bitter" smile that Chillingworth tells the Boston townsman, referring to Hester Prynne's husband, " 'So learned a man as you speak of should have learned this too in his books' " (TSL, p. 62). In his succeeding conversation with Hester in the prison, Chillingworth betrays his suffering by fastening morbidly upon the concrete evidence of his wife's rejection: " 'The child is yours, – she is none of mine, neither will she recognize my voice or aspect as a father's' " (TSL, p. 72). And through Chillingworth's revelation that he feels although " 'Elsewhere a wanderer, and isolated from human interests, ' "he has now found in Boston " ' a woman, a man, a child, amongst whom and myself there exist the closest ligaments' " (TSL, p. 78), Hawthorne exposes the simple cause of the classic cuckold's complicated reaction to adultery: an exclusive dependence on marriage to fill all emotional needs.

In an extremity, Aleksey Aleksandrovich tells Anna, "I am your husband, and I love you" (AK, p. 156). She does not believe him, and we can see why: Nothing in his behavior gives reality to his claim. But although Chillingworth's behavior through the bulk of *The Scarlet Letter* appears as bafflingly heartless as Aleksey Aleksandrovich's, his first conversation with Hester establishes its sufficient emotional basis. Chillingworth never makes Hester an avowal like Aleksey Aleksandrovich's. But having Chillingworth tell her, recalling their married life, " 'I drew thee into my heart, into its innermost chamber, and sought to warm thee by the warmth thy presence made there,' " Hawthorne compels us, with her, to concede that, even in the moral terms of joy and pain that she herself espouses, she " '[has] greatly wronged [him]' " (TSL, p. 74). Masked, inverted, and in a diminished modern world a little absurd, the passion of the novelistic cuckold is recognizable nonetheless: and it is the passion of Othello.

Both *Anna Karenina* and *The Scarlet Letter* testify to the classic phenomenon by which the cuckold steadfastly denies the manifest vindictiveness of his treatment of his wife. As if trying out for *A Woman Killed with Kindness,* Aleksey Aleksandrovich asks Anna sweetly whether she calls it " 'cruelty for a husband to give his wife freedom, giving her the honorable protection of his name, simply on the condition of observing the proprieties?' " But Anna inarticulately feels the charade of his magnanimity: " 'It's worse than cruel — it's base, if you want to know!' " (AK, p. 383). Chillingworth's behavior also displays the characteristic contradiction: Hester, "bewildered and appalled" (TSL, p. 76), cannot at first decide whether his ministrations to her and Pearl in the prison express "humanity or, it may be, a refined cruelty" (TSL, p. 73). But after Chillingworth proceeds dispassionately to elaborate his insane plan of revenge, she confronts him with the discrepancy: " 'Thy acts are like mercy, . . . [but] thy words interpret thee as a terror!' " (TSL, p. 76).

In addition to exposing the passionate impulse behind the cuckold's cold assertions, Hawthorne also accounts for the curious obsession he may develop with his wife's lover. A hypothetic premise of homoeroticism is, it appears, quite unnecessary. Hawthorne makes clear that it is precisely at the moment Hester refuses to identify her lover — the man who, Chillingworth urges, " 'has wronged us both' " — that he makes his avenging vow that " 'Sooner or later, . . . he shall be mine!' " (TSL, pp. 75–6). The connection is plain: Hester, by keeping silent, has shown Chillingworth that she will not be reunited with him on any terms, not even those of vengeance for her own injury. By insisting that it is only when Chillingworth has established the finality of Hester's rejection of them that he turns his attention to her lover, Hawthorne unmasks the cuckold's characteristic obsession with the lover as initially the diverted outlet for his anger at his wife.

Ever since the uxorious Prince de Clèves learned overnight to trick, spy on, and browbeat his wife, it has been a truism in the novel of adultery that the cuckold's reaction to his wife's infidelity transforms his personality.[10] It is this phenomenon Chillingworth is unwittingly articulating when he says of himself, " 'A mortal man, with once a human heart, has become a fiend.' " And Hawthorne goes on to capture the characteristic self-estrangement in a graphic image: " 'the unfortunate physician, while uttering these words, lifted his hands with a look of horror, as if he had beheld some frightful shape, which he could not recognize, usurping the place of his own image in a glass' " (TSL, p. 172). This is no mere gothicism. The "fiend" or, as Aleksey Aleksandrovich experiences it, the "brutal force" (AK, p. 441) impelling these cuckolds to vengeance is the image of their own disinherited humanity come back quite literally to haunt them.

The main reason *The Scarlet Letter* suggests for the cuckold's characteristic lapse into a course of destruction is that he asks too much of his own self-control. Chillingworth claims magnanimously to understand that he and Hester " 'have wronged each other' " (TSL, p. 74). His subsequent behavior, however, broadcasts that the mere recitation of this rational formula did not in fact begin to satisfy his wounded feelings. Hardly a surprise: Self-love alone would reject the idea that his marrying Hester was as bad as her deceiving him.

The case of Chillingworth makes clear that the cuckold's mistake is not his outrage at his wife's infidelity. To feel outraged in his situation is simply nature. To repress the feeling as Chillingworth does in the marketplace, however, is not, and it is that willful denial that is the cause of the cuckold's problem. If by the act of saying " 'Between thee and me, the scale hangs fairly balanced ' " (TSL, p. 75) Chillingworth could make it so, well and good; but the only circumstances under which that statement could genuinely exhaust all the cuckold's reactions would be if he were impervious to rejection – a condition, of course, no human being ever did or could achieve. In the end, Hawthorne shows, although the literary cuckold can force himself to speak rationally, he cannot enforce rationality upon his feelings. And it is for this reason that the reaction to a literary adultery turns out to be at least as anarchic and destructive as the adultery ever was.

3

The hallmark of the classic novel of adultery is its air of doom. The tradition's mortality rate alone seems to confirm Hester Prynne's passionate declaration that " 'There is no good' " for the literary adulteress, her husband, her lover, or even her child — " 'no path to guide [them] out of this dismal maze' " (TSL, p. 173). A short list of the "casualities" of literary adultery would include, most obviously, Emma Bovary, Stendhal's Julien Sorel, Goethe's Ottilie and Eduard, and Chopin's Edna Pontellier; a slightly longer list would add Charles Bovary, Stendhal's Mme. de Rênal, the Prince and Princesse de Clèves, and Rousseau's Julie d'Étanges Wolmar. In addition, the children of Emma, Edna, Julie, and Mme. de Rênal end up orphans, whereas the son of Eduard and Charlotte is drowned. Up to and including Edith Wharton's Newland Archer, no member of a classic adultery triangle ever succeeds in marrying his lover; as Goethe's widowed Charlotte tells her suitor, the Captain, " 'We have done nothing to bring about our unhappiness; but neither have we deserved to be happy together.' "[11]

To be sure, a given adulteress may not, like Emma Bovary, positively commit suicide, nor may her cuckolded husband torment himself, like the Prince de Clèves, positively to death; her children may not end up, like Berthe Bovary, consumptive and in the poorhouse; but their unhappiness is assured nonetheless. From their guilt and grief, the literary adulteress and her companions can expect liberation only from death. According to the novelistic tradition, characters touched by adultery are transported by the fatal act to a region where the novelist himself cannot mitigate their doom. Bold to criticize any historical fashion in morals or manners, the traditional novelist of adultery yet perpetuates unquestioned the ideal of wifely fidelity — a transcendent fixture, the single thing in a secular world that Mystery will still bestir itself to repay. The individual husband (suggests the tradition) and the particular society that harass the adulteress are simply the accidental tools of a supernatural justice.

As much as *Anna Karenina*, *The Scarlet Letter* at first seems to be following the traditional drift. Yet by the time of her conversation with Chillingworth on the seashore, Hester Prynne has had a revolutionary idea. Repudiating her earlier assertion of "no good" (itself probably calculated to manipulate Chillingworth anyway), Hester presses her husband to see that he " '[has] it at [his] will to pardon' " (TSL, p. 174). And although Hester does not look this far, Hawthorne clearly implies that the power she attributes to him belongs in equal measure to her. If Chillingworth can forgive her for her betrayal, she can certainly forgive him for his.

That moral issues are at stake in the literary plot of adultery *The Scarlet Letter* is far from denying, but unlike the novelistic tradition, it locates those issues elsewhere than in the breached commandment. The narrator says of Hester that she "ought long ago to have done" (TSL, p. 177) with the idea that Chillingworth betrayed her; and so indeed, the novel implies, ought *all* the characters to have done with the topic of one another's treachery. It is in the willful refusal to forgive and not in the wound blindly inflicted that Hawthorne suggests we seek the crime in the matter of adultery. In adultery as in every other human situation, Hawthorne insists, nursing an injury loses the injured party any initial moral advantage; indeed, since the intention to retaliate is conscious where the original hurt was unintentional, it actually causes him to sink below the level of his injurer. Insofar as it admitted that vengeance is to be left to the Lord, the tradition had deprecated personal vengefulness; but Hawthorne puts in question the relevance of vengeance altogether.

As Hester pleads to Chillingworth, to end the vicious cycle of injury and vengeance, someone in the adulterous situation must make the effort to renounce his or her private interests in favor of the common weal. Yet even renunciation is not everything. All that renunciation could do, Anna Karenina for one certainly does. On her sickbed, after the birth of her and Vronsky's child, Anna professes remorse for her adultery and requires her husband and her lover to shake hands. Everyone weeps, the sickroom flows with Christian charity, and it seems that all will end well. Yet as Tolstroy documents without analyzing, as soon as Anna begins to mend, she is dismayed to find herself experiencing Aleksey Alek-

147

sandrovich as "insufferably irritating" (AK, p. 445) all over again; and ironically, her very repentance ends by spurring her to the act that, defiant, she had steadfastly refused to perform – deserting her son. It truly seems as if a "hostile demon"[12] (the words of Goethe's Ottilie) foils the adulteress and her companions in their best efforts at self-purification.

The guilt-stricken actors in the classic novel of adultery characteristically struggle to achieve ideal feelings, particularly the Christian feelings of penitence and forgiveness. Hester Prynne's lingering passion for Dimmesdale is something she typically "strove to cast . . . from her" (TSL, p. 80), whereas her hatred for Chillingworth is something for which she "upbraided" herself (p. 176). Like these attempts of Hester's, however, all the conscientious efforts of classic literary adulterers to purify their feelings produce no fruit. While duly recording this phenomenon, *The Scarlet Letter* also suggests a more practical cause than the activity of demons. By the evidence of Hester and Chillingworth, the adulteress's and the cuckold's inability to cast off their ill feeling lies less in moral hardness than in mental confusion.

Mere humanity, *The Scarlet Letter* persuades, might sufficiently explain the adulteress's and the cuckold's incapacity to purely repent, purely forgive; for in the classic plot the grounds on which those acts are asked of them are arbitrary at best and at worst an outrage to their sense of personal justice. The bare Seventh Commandment hardly explains to the classic adulteress *why* she did not have the human right to do anything she could think of to pay back her husband for robbing her of, as she sees it, a woman's one chance for a happy life; yet as Hawthorne shows, the Seventh Commandment is all the classic adulteress is given as a reason to repent. The Sermon on the Mount is far from telling the cuckold why he is not justified in seeking vengeance for the outrage his wife has done his honor, pride, and affections; but again, it is the only incentive he is shown.

If the classic adulteress cannot achieve a sustained penitence, Hawthorne shows, the flaw need not be in her sincere will to do right. The instance of Hester shows that the adulteress may be as sincere as anyone could ask and still simply lack the practical reunderstanding of her situation that successful penitence requires. Like her sisters, Hester can and does try with all her heart to be sorry for having breached a commandment; but because she never intended her affair as a comment upon the decalogue, of course she fails. What the classic adulteress is asked to be sorry for simply does not correspond to what she is conscious of having done. The final reason the conventional religio-moral prescription for adultery is so ineffective, *The Scarlet Letter* shows, is that it leaves the basic emotional issues untouched. It is their attempt to implement ideal solutions before they have identified their real problem that leads classic adulterers into their characteristic confusion. Describing Hester Prynne's attempts to repudiate her own enjoyment of needlework, the narrator, far from applauding her, suggests that "This morbid meddling of conscience with an immaterial matter betokened, it is to be feared, no genuine and steady penitence, but something doubtful, something that might be deeply wrong, beneath" (TSL, p. 84).

The novel of adultery had assumed that marital infidelity must be interpreted in terms of injury. Yet *The Scarlet Letter* suggests that interpreting adultery thus can only cause the husband and wife to paralyze themselves with brooding upon the insoluble question of who injured whom first: whose, in Chillingworth's words, "was the first wrong" (TSL, pp. 74–5). In the name of punishing the appearance of sin, the society that criminalizes adultery may have the effect of creating the actuality. Nor does Hawthorne indicate, nor the tradition bear out, that the Puritans were the only culprits.

Hawthorne is leaving the tradition behind him when he allows Chillingworth to achieve a glimpse of the impropriety of judging the participants within the adulterous situation. Indeed, Hawthorne finally attributes to Hester's husband a more forgiving final position on her adultery than he does to her lover. As the fruit of seven years of contemplation, Chillingworth produces this insight: "'Ye that have wronged me are not sinful, save in a sort of typical illusion; nor am I fiendlike, who have snatched a fiend's office from his hands'" (TSL, p. 175). Having become acquainted with self-willed behavior in his own right, Chillingworth is now able to see that they have been seeking the cause of their sufferings in the wrong place. The germ of their trouble was never in the moral realm. As Chillingworth had already unwittingly suggested by his words in the prison, the mistake was squarely in the realm of nature, in the human world of love and marriage.

It was always clear in the tradition that the adulteress's warrant for her behavior was a treacherous assumption that life owed every woman romantic passion as a universal female birthright. But *The Scarlet Letter* goes on to illuminate a point the tradition had left dark. The example of Chillingworth suggests that, in Hawthorne's analysis, the traditional cuckold must have brought to matrimony a set of overbeliefs of his own, through which he is as deeply implicated in their present catastrophe as his wife.

For Chillingworth's recollections of married life betray that his warrant for insisting on marriage to a girl who had announced she could not love him was his own assumption that life owed every *man* a pleasant domestic arrangement. Indeed, he even imagines that he alone on earth had been invidiously denied this: " 'It was not so wild a dream, – old as I was, and sombre as I was, and misshapen as I was, – that the simple bliss, which is scattered far and wide, for all mankind to share, might yet be mine' " (TSL, p. 74). Recalling his nuptial hopes to Hester, now, after so many vicissitudes, Chillingworth still shows no greater awareness of the breathtaking oversimplifications on which those hopes were based. Even if Chillingworth were safe in supposing that wedded life were always "bliss" – even always "simple" – he still takes the risk of expecting Hester to be an instrument through which his male right to domesticity could be fulfilled. As for her, he vaguely expected that her happiness would follow from his. Now that it turns out that she, like Emma Bovary, had resented the very happiness she gave him, he, like Charles, is for the moment sincerely baffled.

Although Tolstoy also admits that Aleksey Aleksandrovich Karenin took his wife for granted, he betrays no suspicion that this might be a just ground for resentment on her part. Rather, it is made to seem one more variety of the unfortunate behavior, less harmful than Stiva's philandering, that wives must accept. But Hawthorne has Chillingworth himself admit culpability in his behavior. Though long before his feelings can have caught up to his rational words, he tells Hester in the prison:

> I ask not wherefore, nor how, thou has fallen into the pit, or say rather, ascended to the pedestal of infamy on which I found thee. The reason is not far to seek. It was my folly, and thy weakness . . . If sages were ever wise in their own behoof, I might have foreseen all this. I might have known that, as I came out of the vast and dismal forest, and entered this settlement of Christian men, the very first object to meet my eyes would be thyself, Hester Prynne, standing up, a statue of ignominy, before the people. Nay, from the moment when we came down the old church steps, a married pair, I might have beheld the bale-fire of the scarlet letter blazing at the end of our path! (TSL, p. 74)

By itself, of course, this self-punishing recognition is of limited use: If the cuckold-to-be could have thus known himself as such, he could have known to cancel his marriage. Penultimate as it is, however, the insight is more than the typical literary cuckold ever achieves.

And Hawthorne reserves to Chillingworth yet further light. Hester herself can only think to justify her adultery in terms of one particular personal passion, but Chillingworth achieves a larger view. In a powerful irony, it is Chillingworth, not Hester, who comes closest to articulating the antinomian conclusion which the plot of literary adultery had always implied: that a wife's adultery is a revelation not about a woman but about a marriage (and has nothing to do with romantic love). In *The Scarlet Letter*, the cuckolded husband provides the adulteress with the terms of her own vindication: " 'Hadst thou met earlier with a better love than mine,' " Roger Chillingworth sternly instructs Hester, " 'perhaps this evil had not been' " (TSL, p. 173).

Hawthorne does not deny that betrayal is, indeed, at the heart of the adultery plot. But he dissents from the traditional consensus that the most important betrayal is the sexual one. The cases of Chillingworth and Hester show that the husband and wife are victims of more than each other; a myth available on mother's lap, at father's knee, in the playhouse, or in the reading chair has victimized them both. By causing them to develop two mutually exclusive and equally impossible sets of expectations of marriage, their own culture has long since set up both the husband and wife for the injuries they come to do each other as individuals. So long as they insist on holding each other accountable for what was in fact a mutual disappointment, of course they will find no path out of their "dismal maze." And until they recognize the mutuality of their betrayal, the literary cuckold and adulteress cannot escape from the mutual recrimination that traditionally had served them for an effective fate.

The Scarlet Letter is at one with its generic tradition in admitting that marriages, being after all of human devising, can be better and worse made. But in implying that the worse made ones may fail, and that this is an event which it were kinder to provide for than to deny, the novel breaks fresh ground. Considered as a fact of social experience rather than one of transcendent morality or political symbolism, *The Scarlet Letter* suggests, adultery ceases to be an occasion of judgment and becomes an opportunity for charity. As the narrator finally pleads, "To all these shadowy figures, – as well Roger Chillingworth as his companions, – we would fain be merciful" (TSL, p. 260). For as Chillingworth admits, Hester's apparently absentminded breach of the commandment occurred in explicit relation to and was a direct by-product of their ill-conceived marriage.

The revisionistic implications of Hawthorne's interpretation are quickly seen. When the issue of blame is abandoned, the practical question of the adultery situation can finally emerge. Whether the husband and wife are willing to face it or not, the basic question is still, as Stiva puts it, " 'What can be done if a married couple finds that life is impossible for them together?' "

The traditional answer, which Hester Prynne uniquely passes beyond, is that someone or other must magically die. As long as everybody is still alive, however, the situation clearly remains as Stiva describes it: " 'You're wretched, he's wretched, and what good can come of it?' " As Tolstoy's own example of Levin and Kitty amply shows, the merely practical problems of marriage – sex, children, property, in-laws – are difficult enough. Added to them, adherence to a theory of marital indissolubility can only go on to render an honest mistake, like Karenin's or Chillingworth's, a gratuitous lifelong suffering. As thoroughly as Anna Karenina attempts to discredit the suggestion by the suggester, Stiva's own answer to his question arrives with all the force of logic. To insist that death is the only answer, he holds, his sister is simply being melodramatic and stubborn: " 'When divorce would solve everything' " (AK, p. 449).

Whether it fits anyone's theory or not, it is clear that although it is given to the literary adulteress and cuckold to pardon each other, their forgiveness will endure only if their sufferings are brought to an end. By the device of Anna's flight from Karenin's house after receiving his forgiveness, even Tolstoy tacitly acknowledges the impossibility of the classic adulteress and the classic cuckold's continuing to live together. The main reason Hester and Chillingworth move so far toward forgiveness as they do is clearly not that either of them is of superior moral fiber, but that Hawthorne has arranged that forgiveness in their situation does not imply that they must resume living together.

In the Roman Catholic settings of the mainstream tradition − *The Princesse de Clèves, Red and Black, Madame Bovary, The Awakening* − historical social institutions prevented the novelist from giving his characters any practical option except to try, impossibly, to resume or continue living together; yet because the *donnee* of the plot is that this is what they cannot do, the classic ending of a novel of adultery became indeed, as Anna says, death. And because of the characters' real lack of choices, the central French tradition is authentically tragic. In a setting that permits divorce, however, if the characters end as sadly as their predecessors, it must be by someone's free choice. With *Elective Affinities,* the novel of adultery modulated from tragedy to irony. *The Scarlet Letter* is at the center of this development; *Anna Karenina* is a denial of it.

4

It is not necessary to know that Tolstoy was a reader of Hawthorne (on at least one occasion sending a magazine the translation of a Hawthorne story)[13] to suspect that *Anna Karenina* is a retort to *The Scarlet Letter.* The likeness of the Karenins' married life to the Amsterdam days of Hester and Chillingworth seems too close for mere coincidence. And when Anna and Vronsky escape to Venice, they seem to be following Hester's plan for a flight to "pleasant Italy" (TSL, p. 197).

Whether an adulterous couple can by any means make a workable life for themselves and their children is a question *The Scarlet Letter* leaves open, but one that a major purpose of Tolstoy's seems to have been to close. By showing Vronsky and Anna, given every chance, yet failing to find happiness, Tolstoy appears to wish to clarify what was in *The Scarlet Letter*, to say the least, unclear: that adulterers always come to bad ends. As his epigraph proclaims, it is his purpose to demonstrate that, however sadly understandable, however painfully pitiable the situation of the individual adulterer, the relevant fact in the case – in Hawthorne, dangerously obscured – is finally only one: "Thou shalt not commit adultery," and the Old Testament God will repay. Distracted by Hester's charms, Hawthorne was clearly too sympathetic to what Edith Wharton would call "the dread argument of the individual case."[14] But although Tolstoy gives the devil her due, he nonetheless destroys her.

The problem with Tolstoy's position – and he is the most blatant novelist of adultery to invoke absolute standards of "right" and "wrong" (AK, p. 449) – is obvious. Although his morality requires the adulteress and cuckold to remain together, his art knows this is humanly impossible. Tolstoy explicitly urges the reader to pin his hopes on the successful marriage of Levin and Kitty. But it is not only glaringly obvious that just as Mme. Homais is no Emma Bovary, Kitty is no Anna; the marriage itself is essentially different. Tolstoy establishes that Kitty and Levin are close in age, made their own choices of each other, and had all their romantic illusions over with before marriage. Such a fortunate marriage is perfectly possible, but it hardly helps with the problem of the less fortunate ones. If every marriage were like that of Levin and Kitty, the novel of adultery would never have developed in the first place.

Hester Prynne more than once considers killing herself and Pearl too. Dimmesdale tells her not to, and she ends, to her own surprise, living a long, healthy, and rather interesting international life – certainly a far more independent and original one than any she could have shared with either Roger Chillingworth or Arthur Dimmesdale. And in the end, not even the illegitimate Pearl suffers any lasting blight.

154

By insisting that Hester survives and that Pearl finds happiness, Hawthorne had unleashed the possibility that the grim fortune of the classic adulteress was just that: fortune, not fate. But if the adulteress's traditional death is not, after all, a consequence of her adultery, it must be a consequence of something else; if fate is not to blame, then something closer to home must be. By the time she commits suicide the classic adulteress is certainly insane, but what made her so? Was Emma, Emma (Hawthorne helps us ask) when she grasped the arsenic? Who really killed Madame Bovary?

If Hawthorne's comprehensive naturalism quietly undermines the somber tradition that disaster is simply the organic blossoming of the "black flower" (TSL, p. 174) of adultery, *Anna Karenina* appears calculated to reestablish it. Where Hester lives to theorize about the relation between the sexes and to counsel the women of Boston, Anna Karenina throws herself under a train. Where Hester and her companions achieve a sorrowful mutual for-giveness on the occasion of Dimmesdale's (nonsuicidal) death, Anna and Vronsky are finally as much estranged as Anna and Karenin; rather than fostering reconciliation, Anna's death causes Vronsky to seek his own death in battle in order to regain his self-respect. Where Pearl lives to find her happy ending, little Annie, left motherless, is snatched from her playboy father by her late mother's estranged husband for an unforeseeable future. At every point where Hawthorne seems to leave a loophole, Tolstoy steps in forcibly to close it.

If Tolstoy found *The Scarlet Letter*'s naturalism threatening, he was not the first. "In Hawthorne's tale," the Reverend Arthur Cleveland Coxe had railed for a whole constituency in 1850, "the lady's frailty is philosophized into a natural and necessary result of the Scriptural law of marriage, which, by holding her irrevocably to her vows, as plighted to a dried-up old bookworm, in her silly girlhood, is viewed as making her heart a too-easy victim to the adulterer."[15] And indeed, in no consideration than that of his refusal to cast Hester into the blackness of darkess is Hawthorne further from the traditional novel of adultery.

Like Flaubert, Tolstoy progressively distances us from the char-acter of the adulteress. He exaggerates Anna's jealousy, her ill temper, her coquetry, and suggests a positive viciousness in her lack of interest in her and Vronsky's child, her dependence on morphine, her smoking, and her use of birth control. Like Flaubert, adding insult to injury, he even stipulates that a woman under the influence of adultery grows fat.[16] In general, he simply heaps up Anna's mounting eccentricities until, although we can still pity her – as the Boston townspeople pity Hester, from comfortably far off – we no longer in the least identify with her. Anna safely dead, Tolstoy invites us to renew the hypothetical possibility (clearly too dangerous to raise while she was alive) that her actions might possibly have been justified. Pleasurable although it is, however, shedding tears over Anna's corpse hardly substitutes for doing justice to her position. His killing Anna finally confirms that Tolstoy has no rational account – or at least none he is willing to give – of adultery as a practical marital and social issue. Throwing Anna under the train, Tolstoy simply throws up that problem.

Tolstoy's cavalier commingling of symbolic mysteries with novelistic realism betrays the wishful fabulousness of his plot. Like Emma Bovary with her blind beggar, Anna is tormented by symbolic manifestations.[17] She and Vronsky are both terrified by dreams in which a hideous peasant mumbles unintelligible French (AK, pp. 375–6, 381). Given the slightest encouragement we would snicker, but Tolstoy is all too pious. That there was something inherently fatal in Anna's and Vronsky's connection from the beginning, *Anna Karenina* positively insists. Anna herself interprets the suicide that occurs at their first meeting in the train station as an "evil omen" (AK, p. 71) – and Tolstoy undertakes to bear her out.

Orthodox preference notwithstanding, Hawthorne allows no magic dreams and no symbolic beggars in *The Scarlet Letter* – not even so much as an ironic golden bowl. *Anna Karenina* upholds Anna's superstitions; but if Dimmesdale sees an **A** in the sky, or if certain Boston townspeople see **A** on his chest, that is strictly their business: "the reader may choose," and one of the choices is none of the above. If he were not merely to encourage readers to congratulate themselves on their own superior morality, the novelist of adultery, Hawthorne saw, had a particular need to eschew the kinds of fantastic effects that would seem to put the characters beyond what Hawthorne insists is a universal fellowship of "human frailty and sorrow" (TSL, p. 48).

The signal difference between Hawthorne and the authors of the mainstream tradition is that where the tendency of their storytelling is to perpetuate the same social institutions whose ill effects furnish them with their material, his is ultimately to put in question those institutions themselves. For where the perpetuation of their tragic tradition depends on the preservation of the unhappiness of the status quo, he makes it clear that he does not assume that tragedy is the only worthy dramatic form. As it is, he gives *The Scarlet Letter* the happiest ending he can; and he would clearly have given it a happier one if historical conditions – not only those of his setting but also of his literary audience – had permitted. If morality certainly consisted in the pretense of immediate, visible punishment for the breaking of cultural taboos, then Arthur Cleveland Coxe was right: *The Scarlet Letter* is an immoral book. But if morality had anything to do with justice to the individual, Hawthorne might have felt that his was the first novel of adultery to begin to be moral at all.

NOTES

1 Q. D. Leavis, "Hawthorne as Poet," *Sewanee Review* 59 (Summer 1951): 426–58. For other comparisons of Hawthorne and Tolstoy, see William Dean Howells, *Heroines of Fiction*, excerpted in Kermit Vanderbilt, ed., *The Achievement of William Dean Howells* (Princeton, N.J.: Princeton University Press, 1968), p. 75; and Earl H. Rovit, "Ambiguity in Hawthorne's *Letter*," in Arlin Turner, ed., *Merrill Studies in the Scarlet Letter* (Columbus, Ohio: Merrill, 1970), p. 121.

2 By the "novel of adultery," I understand the tradition discussed by Tony Tanner in *Adultery in the Novel* (Baltimore: Johns Hopkins University Press, 1979) and Judith Armstrong in *The Novel of Adultery* (New York: Barnes and Noble, Import Division of Harper & Row, 1976) including such works as La Fayette's *Princesse de Clèves*, Rousseau's *Julie*, Goethe's *Elective Affinities*, Stendhal's *The Red and the Black*, Flaubert's *Madame Bovary*, and Kate Chopin's *The Awakening*. For Tanner, who proposes a tentative syllabus for the genre in a foot-

note (p. 12), the central texts in the tradition are *Madame Bovary, Elective Affinities,* and *Julie.* For Armstrong, *Madame Bovary, Anna Karenina,* and James's *Golden Bowl* are the indispensable works (p. 169). Without undertaking a discussion, Tanner identifies *The Scarlet Letter* as "Hawthorne's novel of adultery" (p. 357); Armstrong gives a brief reading (pp. 101–4) that essentially repeats the "love and death" interpretation of Leslie Fiedler.

3 Quotations from *Anna Karenina* are taken from the Constance Garnett translation, rev. Leonard J. Kent and Nina Berberova (New York: Modern Library, 1965).

4 Emma Bovary, for one, does this constantly, but especially in the episode with the clubfoot; see *Madame Bovary,* edited with a substantially new translation by Paul de Man (New York: Norton, 1965), p. 133.

5 See, for instance, *Madame Bovary,* p. 122; cf. *Elective Affinities,* trans. Elizabeth Mayer and Louise Bogan (South Bend, Indiana: Gateway Editions, 1963), p. 261.

6 See *Madame Bovary,* p. 133.

7 *The Princesse de Clèves* spells out the fact that Mlle. de Chartres's marriage is a political arrangement made by her mother; in addition, Mme. de Lafayette makes clear that, as Mlle. de Chartres admits, the bride "was not particularly attracted by [her husband's] person"; see *The Princesse de Clèves,* trans. Nancy Mitford (New York: Penguin Books, 1978), p. 47. And in *Red and Black,* Stendhal's narrator explains that Mme. de Rênal is given in marriage to her older husband straight from the convent, without having any idea what love is; see *Red and Black,* trans. Robert M. Adams (New York: Norton, 1969), p. 35.

8 See especially *The Princesse de Clèves,* pp. 130–40, 147–50, 166, 174–8.

9 See *Madame Bovary,* p. 29, and passim.

10 The Prince de Clèves sets the pattern of the cuckold whose unrestrained jealously becomes, literally, the death of him; see *The Princesse de Clèves,* pp. 174–8.

11 *Elective Affinities,* p. 267.

12 Ibid., p. 288.

13 *Tolstoy's Letters,* selected, edited, and translated by R. F. Christian, 2 vols. (New York: Scribners, 1978), vol. 2, p. 464.

14 Edith Wharton, *The Age of Innocence* (New York: Scribners, 1968), p. 309.

15 The *Scarlet Letter* section of Coxe's "The Writings of Hawthorne"

(*Church Review*, vol. 3, January 1851) was reprinted by A. Mordell in *Notorious Literary Attacks* (New York, 1926). The present quotation is drawn from the Norton Critical *Scarlet Letter*, ed. Sculley Bradley, Richmond Croom Beatty, E. Hudson Long, and Seymour Gross, 2nd ed. (New York: Norton, 1978), p. 258.

16 On Anna's jealousy, see, for instance, pp. 769, 772; on her ill temper, pp. 734–5; on her morphine addiction, pp. 668–9, 697; on her co-quetry, pp. 659–60, 726–30, 733; on her lack of interest in her child, pp. 646–7, 696; on her smoking, p. 726; on her use of birth control, p. 666; and on her weight gain, p. 378. Cf. *Madame Bovary*, pp. 138, 140, and Chopin's *The Awakening* (Toms River, N.J.: Capricorn Books, 1964), p. 216. To judge from the literary tradition, adultery is illegal, immoral, *and* fattening.

17 For Emma's beggar, see *Madame Bovary*, pp. 193, 219, 238. It almost seems that the mysterious beggar is an obligatory feature in a novel of adultery: cf. Goethe, *Elective Affinities*, pp. 55–6, 127. As Anna Karenina's death seems foreshadowed by the suicide in the train station at her meeting with Vronsky, so the drowning of Goethe's adulterers' infant son is foreshadowed by several drowning or near-drownings: see pp. 34, 99, 117–18, 241–4. There are a plethora of other supernatural or symbolic manifestations in *Elective Affinities* as well; see, for instance, pp. 75, 114.

Notes on Contributors

Michael Davitt Bell is J. Leland Miller Professor of American History, Literature, and Eloquence at Williams College, where he teaches courses in English and American Studies. Besides his many contributions to scholarly journals, he is the author of a significant study of Hawthorne's literary text: *Hawthorne and the Historical Romance of New England*. His most recent book is *The Development of American Romance: The Sacrifice of Relation*.

Carol Bensick is Assistant Professor of English and American Studies at the University of Oregon. In addition to a revisionist essay on "Hawthorne's Humor," forthcoming in a volume of essays from the 1984 Penn State Conference on American Comedy, she is the author of *La Nouvelle Beatrice*, a study of the "historicity" of "Rappaccini's Daughter."

Michael J. Colacurcio has taught American literary and intellectual history at Cornell University for over twenty years; he is currently Professor of English and American Studies at the University of California, Los Angeles. He is the author of *The Province of Piety: Moral History in Hawthorne's Early Tales*.

David Van Leer is the Andrew W. Mellon Assistant Professor of English and American Studies at Princeton University. In addition to a variety of essays and reviews, he has written a major study of Emerson's career and achievement as a philosopher — *Emerson's Epistemology*, forthcoming (1986) from Cambridge University Press.

161

Selected Bibliography

All references to the text of *The Scarlet Letter* in the foregoing essays are to Volume I of *The Centenary Edition of the Works of Nathaniel Hawthorne* (Columbus: Ohio State University Press, 1962). This carefully established text has been widely reprinted – in the Library of America Series, for example, and in many useful paperbacks – but the *Centenary* remains the standard for citation in scholarly books and articles.

The following selection of critical works does not attempt to provide a comprehensive listing of the (prolific) scholarship on *The Scarlet Letter*. And although most of the works discussed in the Introduction are cited in full here, the purpose is not to specify the materials from which to reinvent that developmental survey. Listed below are merely some judiciously selected works for further reading – for the student who wishes to begin to explore "the best that has been thought and said" about the subject of this volume. (Additional bibliographic materials are given in footnote 4 to the Introduction.)

Abel, Darrel. "Hawthorne's Dimmesdale: Fugitive from Wrath." *Nineteenth-Century Fiction* 11 (September 1956):81–105.

Baym, Nina. *The Shape of Hawthorne's Career.* Ithaca, N.Y.: Cornell University Press, 1975.

Becker, John E. *Hawthorne's Historical Allegory.* Port Washington, N.Y.: Kennikat Press, 1971.

Bell, Michael Davitt. *Hawthorne and the Historical Romance of New England.* Princeton, N.J.: Princeton University Press, 1971.

Bell, Millicent. "The Obliquity of Signs: *The Scarlet Letter,*" *Massachusetts Review* 23 (Spring 1982):9–26.

Carpenter, Frederic I. "Scarlet A Minus," *College English* 5 (January 1944):173–80.

Chase, Richard. *The American Novel and Its Tradition.* Garden City, N.Y.: Doubleday, 1957.

Colacurcio, Michael J. "The Footsteps of Ann Hutchinson," *ELH* 39 (September 1972):459–94.

Crews, Frederick. *The Sins of the Fathers*. New York: Oxford University Press, 1966.

Davidson, Edward H. "Dimmesdale's Fall," *New England Quarterly* 26 (September 1963):358–70.

Feidelson, Charles. "*The Scarlet Letter*," in R. H. Pearce, ed. *Hawthorne Centenary Essays*. Columbus: Ohio State University Press, 1964.

Fogle, Richard Harter. *Hawthorne's Fiction: The Light and the Dark*. Norman: University of Oklahoma Press, 1952.

Gerber, John C. "Form and Content in *The Scarlet Letter*," *New England Quarterly* 17 (March 1944):25–55.

Gross, Seymour L. "Solitude, and Love, and Anguish," *CLA Journal* 3 (March 1968):154–65.

Hansen, Elaine T. "Ambiguity and the Narrator in *The Scarlet Letter*," *Journal of Narrative Technique* 5 (September 1975):147–63.

James, Henry. *Hawthorne*. London: Macmillan, 1879. (Reprinted Ithaca, N.Y.: Cornell University Press, 1967).

Lawrence, D. H. *Studies in Classic American Literature*. New York: T. Seltzer, 1923. (Reprinted Garden City, N.Y.: Doubleday, 1951).

Leverenz, David. "Mrs. Hawthorne's Headache: Reading *The Scarlet Letter*," *Nineteenth-Century Fiction* 37 (March 1983):552–75.

McCall, Dan. "The Design of Hawthorne's 'Custom-House,'" *Nineteenth-Century Fiction* 21 (March 1967):349–58.

McNamara, Anne Marie. "The Character of Flame: The Function of Pearl in *The Scarlet Letter*," *American Literature* 27 (January 1956):537–53.

Male, Roy R. *Hawthorne's Tragic Vision*. Austin: University of Texas Press, 1957.

Matthiessen, F. O. *American Renaissance*. New York: Oxford University Press, 1941.

Rowe, John Carlos. "The Internal Conflict of Romantic Narrative," *Modern Language Notes* 95 (December 1980):1203–31.

Ryskamp, Charles. "The New England Sources of *The Scarlet Letter*," *American Literature* 31 (November 1959):257–72.

Sandeen, Ernest. "*The Scarlet Letter* as a Love Story," *PMLA* 77 (September 1962):425–35.

Turner, Arlin. *Nathaniel Hawthorne: A Biography*. New York: Oxford University Press, 1980.

Waggoner, Hyatt H. *Hawthorne: A Critical Study*. Cambridge, Mass.: Harvard University Press, 1955.

Warren, Austin. "*The Scarlet Letter*: A Literary Exercise in Moral Theology," *Southern Review* 1 (1965):22–45.